TRAVELS IN THE CITIES OF CINEMA

TRAVELS IN THE CITIES OF CINEMA

Jonathan Rosenbaum

Conversations with
Ehsan Khoshbakht

Sticking Place Books
New York

© Jonathan Rosenbaum and Ehsan Khoshbakht 2025
© Sticking Place Books 2025

www.stickingplacebooks.com

Cover image: Jonathan Rosenbaum in front of Frank Lloyd Wright's Robie House in Chicago. Photo © Mehrnaz Saeed-Vafa.

All rights reserved.

No part of this book may be reproduced, stored in or introduced into a retrieval system, or transmitted, in any form or by any means (electronic, mechanical, photocopying, recording or otherwise) without the written permission of the publishers, except in the case of brief quotations embodied in critical articles or reviews.

ISBN 978-1-942782-88-9

CONTENTS

Introduction	vii
Prelude: Digital Encounters	1
Florence	7
New York and the 1960s	27
Paris	35
London	45
Back to the U.S.A.	69
Chicago	91
Critic as Artist	139
Appendix: Jonathan Rosenbaum's Favorite Jazz Recordings	163
Bibliography	165
Index	167

INTRODUCTION

I have talked on many occasions to American film critic Jonathan Rosenbaum, whom I regard as one of the finest film critics in the English-speaking world: over meals, over emails, while strolling in the streets of London, Bologna, Cambridge and Istanbul, in panel discussions and joint introductions to screenings. Jonathan and I have collaborated in multiple capacities as co-writers, co-curators, fellow travelers and even as filmmakers. For this book, however, I tried to set aside all I knew and begin at the beginning.

Here, our discussion revolves around *him*, which means mostly talking about cinema as a kind of "News on the March." Jonathan, the author of numerous books on cinema and a professional critic since the 1970s who has appeared on the juries of numerous film festivals, and on panel discussions and in documentaries, is very much an archivist of his own work. From early on, he began compiling his writings—some of which date as far back as the 1950s—on his own website, making his extensive body of work freely accessible to readers.

Complementing his website, this book serves as an archive of the man himself. Yet, even within his extensive body of writings—from film criticism to literary criticism and commentary on music, politics and people—a sizeable degree of autobiography has always been apparent. My approach here is to take his writings as cues, weaving them together and filling in the gaps by encouraging him to reflect on topics he has not previously articulated, at least not within the public sphere.

The fragments of a Rosenbaum I once knew have now coalesced into a more complete portrait in words, shaped partly by him and partly by the direction in which I steered this conversation. In doing so, I inevitably imposed some of my own subjectivity, to which he variously acquiesced, resisted or countered. At times, he refrains from directly answering a question I pose. I have resisted the temptation to revise those questions for the sake of appearance; they remain as originally asked.

I have kept the conversation largely in the order in which it unfolded, with minimal editing beyond some necessary refinements made by both of us. The flow and sequencing remain faithful to the original exchanges that took place during the autumn and early winter of 2024.

To avoid redundancy, I have drawn selectively from two earlier conversations—one on jazz, the other on Abbas Kiarostami, both of which are available in their entirety on his website—and integrated these elements into the text. Repeating those discussions in detail felt unnecessary, as they had already been thoroughly explored.

The chapters of this book are organized around the cities where Jonathan has lived and worked: Florence, New York, Paris, London and Chicago. Of these, Chicago has now been his home for longer than any other; it is where he has lived since 1987. It is also the city where he embarked on—and ultimately retired from—the longest-running position of his career, as chief film critic for the *Chicago Reader*, an alternative weekly, from 1987 to 2008.

One city, absent from the map, yet central to my discovery of Jonathan and his work, is the Internet, an imaginary geographical network that first connected us and that has since become dystopian. Through his website, and as far back as the days of dial-up Internet, he became one of the first film critics I read regularly, sometimes even daily, while I was still living in Mashhad, Iran. (Like Jonathan, I later moved to London, though, unlike him, I adapted better to its weather, which is why I stayed.)

I believe there is a particular advantage to his post-*Reader* writing and its Internet reincarnation: he is no longer obliged to tailor his insights to an "average American reader," a task that often required him to clarify and challenge preconceptions. Freed from such constraints, the Internet and his internationalism have allowed his writing to transcend geographic boundaries. He no longer needs to fill the gaps of ignorance—whether historical or aesthetic—that so often frustrated him. Following the *Reader* period, he has spoken to those who have some common ground with him and a reasonable grasp of film history. This has made him a niche writer. But I prefer the "niche Rosenbaum" to his other incarnations.

It was through one of Jonathan's dispatches about an Italian film festival called Il Cinema Ritrovato that I was inspired to attend the event, held in the city of Bologna. There, in June 2012, I not only met him for the first time in the physical world but, in time, found myself co-directing the festival. In a sense, it was Jonathan who illuminated the path.

I have found as much joy in his company as in his writing. His optimism and boundless energy are deeply inspiring, particularly at a time when many critics of his generation no longer find it inspiring to be a critic. What I admire most about his attitude towards life is that he never says "No." While "No" is most often the easiest way out, he opts for the collective, the joyful that lies in "Yes." With Jonathan, there is always time for one more film, one more good meal.

Jonathan's use of first-person criticism and the strong presence of "I" in his writing has sometimes been misconstrued as self-centred. However, I value this quality, as it clarifies his position and openly acknowledges the limitations and biases of the speaker. In his latest publication, *In Dreams Begin Responsibilities*, he rightly detects the absence of "I" in the ostensibly first-person documentaries of Adam Curtis, which disguise themselves otherwise, and through the deliberate omission of "I" allow rhetorical tricks to be sold as conclusive demonstration of facts. I have also been troubled—though to a much lesser extent—by the writings of Jonathan's former housemate, the erudite Raymond Durgnat, in his seminal *A Mirror for England* (1970), in which he oddly decided to use "we" (= England) instead of the "I" that he is or was.

This "I" in Jonathan's work also bears a connection to jazz. I have referred to him as a "bebop film critic" simply because he "bops it."* Allow me to explain, without delving into technicalities:

Much like the works of bebop musicians, Jonathan's writing is rooted in a collective experience—one performer responding to the work of another. Many of his writings emerge from a dynamic where the critic's role is partially built upon preexisting frameworks, whether correct or

---

* Bebop or bop was a revolutionary phase in jazz history that emerged during WWII from the intimate, informal jam sessions among friends and competitors in New York as a reaction to jazz being too formulated, too commercial and too hidebound to serve as dance music. In order to go beyond these confines, a wider range of harmonic possibilities were explored and unusual melodies, in which chord changes were what mattered most to the musicians, were jazzed. Usually the melodic line was stated and then kicked out the window to make room for extended, play-or-die solos. It was a conversational, often fast-paced and aggressive urban music with a sophistication that was sometimes too "new" for its time.

flawed, that shape the discourse that precedes his arguments.

There is an element of improvisation in his work, and as with all improvisation, it carries an air of excitement and unpredictability, even when it falls short. (I recall one instance when, during a joint introduction to a film, we decided to improvise on stage. On that occasion, I believe our experiment was not entirely successful.)

Despite the speed and spontaneity of his approach—a quality very much in the spirit of bebop—Jonathan's polemics and phrasing remain remarkably clear and incisive.

Like bebop musicians, Jonathan seeks to provoke, though not invariably. He is also notably kinder to his "bandmates" than to the soloists of other bands.

His writing, much like bebop compositions, is deeply personal and laced with secret codes and references, nods to people and situations that are not always immediately decipherable to everyone. Charlie Parker's joyous "Moose the Mooche," for instance, was a covert homage to his pusher. In this book, Jonathan acknowledges at least one such coded reference in his own writings: an allusion to Manny Farber.

Occasionally, as with some jazz artists, a bit of chemical stimulation lends its assistance. In Jonathan's case, it is strictly marijuana.

He repeats things, but these repetitions are presented as new variations, much like when Charlie Parker introduces a phrase in "Hootie Blues," repeats it in a different key in "Lady Be Good," and then in "Billie's Bounce," yet again in another key. I have, in this book, preserved these repeated phrases because, to me, they are in different keys. He also demonstrates a bebop sensibility in his treatment of riffs, reconfiguring his old texts for new purposes.

Jonathan shows an openness to form and employs various formats in criticism, from epistolary to formalist, from reportage to Hegelian dissection. Most recently, when I commissioned him to write about Andre De Toth's career at Columbia Pictures, his submission surprised me. It was framed as an investigative piece, a form of detective work that unraveled a misremembrance by Bertrand Tavernier of a scene in a De Toth film. Through this exploration, Jonathan explains why De Toth's cinema can often lead to such confusion.

He occasionally gets "bluesy," addressing the injustices faced by the subjects of his writing. At times, he also reflects on the injustices he himself has endured.

Much like bebop musicians' historical references in their playing, Jonathan's writing is rich with citations and references to cinema, and writings by others (hence the lengthy quotes in some of his criticism). Very often these writings can get self-referential as well.

For him, a piece of criticism is never a static entity. It is a continuation of something begun by him or another, with the hope that it will evolve into something else in the future, linking to new ideas and connecting with other work. In this sense, Jonathan is a mediator between texts, ideas and things.

In this book, I aim to preserve that sense of free association between cultural and political elements as a core part of our conversation. In attention to daily, almost insignificant details, I wanted the dialogue to resemble an Ozu film, while as an instant reaction to the world around us through fragments of images and texts, I was thinking of Godard's collages.

Now, let me ask him the first question.

Ehsan Khoshbakht
London, January 2025

Jonathan Rosenbaum and Ehsan Khoshbakht in Ankara, in front of the poster for their "Jazz Goes to the Movies" program. Photo © Ahmet Gürata.

PRELUDE: DIGITAL ENCOUNTERS

I wanted to start by discussing the medium we are using. We have, over the years, met in person on many occasions, but digital technology is what connected us 16 years ago and has been the format for many of our past conversations. How has this technology, and its impact on your life, changed for you over the past two decades?

I have mixed feelings about it. On the one hand, I owe most of my national and international reputation to the fact that the *Chicago Reader* set up a website shortly after I became their film critic in 1987, which is how you were able to discover me while you were still living in Iran and could send me emails correcting typos and suggesting better stills to run with my reviews. This was even before the *Reader* established my own website, when I retired from the paper in 2008.

One example of the negative side of this technology is that most people I know used to have their friends' phone numbers memorized, but today that is less likely because we expect the machine to do it all for us, and as a consequence, we know less. We are more disabled because of it. This happens in all kinds of ways. It is even a theme of the book that I just finished writing, *Camera Movements That Confound Us*. One thing I can add that is very disturbing is that I think people now try to imitate machines. It's almost like machines are held in higher regard than people, and people aspire to the precision of machines. One of the things that also disturbs me is that if you look on the Internet at things that just appear as emails and so on of people posting, they all seem to be imitating each other, writing in the same inflated style, the same language, so you can't even tell if it's AI or a real person who is responsible. But it really doesn't matter because even if it's a person, it's a person trying to imitate a machine.

Would you say that your initial optimism about the new horizons opened up by digital technology has faded, and that digital possibilities are beginning to consume themselves?

There's always been a double edge to the technology. It has led to a lot of confusion because people have too easy an escape clause. If anything goes wrong, no one takes responsibility for it; they say it's the fault of the algorithms. But, of course, it's *people* who make the decisions about the algorithms. I think one of the plagues of modern life today is what I would call capitalist censorship, which basically rules a lot of things out of our lives, even though we think it's all based on our free will. What we have is a situation where mankind as a whole is like the left hand that doesn't know what the right hand is doing, and vice versa. Our momentary desires, which we sometimes may not even be fully conscious or aware of, are what TV is based on—gratifying or at least stimulating those desires. In fact, it's usually against gratifying them because if it's gratified, then you wouldn't want to buy more goods. It's about appealing to our baser instincts, and that's constantly determining what's in the news. In other words, the news tends to prefer disasters to good news, anything that gets the heart racing. It's all about getting more people to spend more money. We pretend there's some kind of objectivity when basically there's only the desire of tycoons to make more money, which they don't need anyway and which they stupidly claim is the "desire" of the algorithms.

You have made friends in this digital world, and you have lost friends in it as well. Are we living in an age of digital intolerance, where people are less open online than they are in real life?

Sure. I think there are ways that people can hide on the Internet, which makes things even worse. We used to have at least the illusion of an objective index to things that we could point to and say: this is real and this is not. But when we don't have that anymore, it puts us all at a disadvantage. I think it's a real problem, but the point is that we're in a situation where even to address the situation we're in is impossible if we're under the control of capitalist censorship. And this has affected me in all kinds of ways. For instance, *In Dreams Begin Responsibilities* is a book that was twice accepted or almost accepted, basically submitted to university presses whose editors liked it but whose publicists vetoed it. The fact that American university presses can have publicists who are more powerful than the editors is already a sign of what's wrong with the culture.

Do you think the widespread availability of films has created a state of confusion due to their abundance and the lack of guidance on how to engage with them? Personally, I feel that I need fewer images—fewer images that allow me to spend more time digesting and understanding them.

That makes sense, and maybe it's relevant that I'm currently in the process of selling my own digital film collection. Part of this is to pay off debts. I've run up credit card debts and borrowed a lot of money from my sister-in-law, and I want to pay her back.

Also, I realize that there's so much you can get one way or another, either on pirate sites or just on YouTube. Even though it's not always the ideal way of seeing it, I find that as a critic, I'm less of a purist than a lot of my colleagues. Most of the films I watch, I watch on my laptop. This is not about the question of power that you just mentioned, but about the lack of cohesion in the world that we live in.

Orson Welles addressed this in F for Fake: *the lack of a point of reference, where there are simply too many mirrors, makes it impossible to discern which is the reflection and which is the real thing.*

One of the things that is confusing philosophically or metaphysically is that we grew up with the idea that there was a commonly held fund of information—things that we could all agree on. That's what is being thrown into question now. In other words, the idea of consensus, that there are areas of agreement between people. And so we don't know whether to regard Donald Trump as a showbiz character or a politician. A lot of people may think, "Okay, agreed, he's a blight on humanity, but at the same time, he's a great sitcom character." In other words, if people wind up voting for him, it's because they are voting for a sitcom character, not a president. They figure they spend most of their time watching television anyway, so it's more relevant to their experience to have a sitcom character in their living room that they prefer than to have a president that they prefer.

When that happens, there is no longer an agreed-upon reality. In other words, either you think that life is like a TV show or you don't. But the whole point of Trump's candidacy is based on the conviction that a TV show is more important than a political policy. To be entertained is the priority. If people like Trump, it's not because they think he's a good politician; it's because they are somehow entertained by him.

You were one of the first critics to transition to the digital world by starting your own website. Now, however, you spend more time working on books, including the one that forms the basis of our current conversation, rather than producing new content for your website. Do you think this return to the book format reflects a rejection of some of the confusion inherent in the digital universe?

I wonder about that. One of the unusual things about *In Dreams Begin Responsibilities* is that it's weighted much more towards the present than towards the past, even though it's in chronological order, because I published so many of my earlier pieces in previous collections. In other words, I feel like there's an awful lot in this book that represents me today, since I retired from the *Chicago Reader.*

I actually think the big difference is that when I was working for the *Reader*, every time I went to a movie, it was a matter of course that I would always have to see it to the end, whether I liked it or not. There was a lot of alienated labor in the sense that I had to devote a lot of my time to films that I wouldn't have wanted to see if it had been left up to me as a consumer. Now it's completely different. If something doesn't grab me right away, I'll go to something else. As a consequence, my whole perspective has changed.

What are you currently working on?

On Monday I'm going to see the new Francis Coppola film, *Megalopolis*, because I'm reviewing it for *Sight and Sound.* Then I have to write the review in 24 hours. That's another example of how the industry controls information flow and reviews in a certain way by not allowing people a longer lead time. I'm not sure how I feel about this because I don't mind having a short lead time. Sometimes it helps to focus me. One of my favorite pieces in my new book is on Godard, which was written within 24 hours from the time I got the news that he died to the time that I had to submit it.

Why do you accept assignments like the Megalopolis *review for* Sight and Sound *when the pay won't help your finances and when publishing something on your own website would potentially reach as many people?*

Because I still like to believe that I'm part of a community. It's a question of speaking to members of my community.

FLORENCE

You were born in Florence, Alabama. What kind of town was that?

It's atypical of Alabama because the Tennessee Valley Authority, which was started during the Depression as part of the New Deal, was built there. So it did have—I don't know if it still has—the cheapest electricity in the country. And partly because of that there's more influx of people from outside the South and even outside the U.S. There are areas in Alabama where there are more black people than white people. But in Florence, the black population is only about 20% or 25%.

Did Rosenbaums have a long history there?

My father lived in Florence since he was ten years old, in 1920, but my grandfather was from Lublin, Poland. He came over to the States when he was 16 or so. In his teens he lived in different places before going to Florence, but he had already gotten involved with movie theaters, I think originally in Nebraska and then in Little Rock, Arkansas, where my father had dim memories of going to see *Intolerance*. And then he came to Florence.

My family could be described as intellectual and politically liberal. My grandfather was a very admired and even beloved philanthropist in my hometown. He paid for not only a large section of the local library, but also made a large contribution toward building a Christian church. In other words, he actually helped people in all sorts of ways, and not in any tribal way, but much more as a kind of universalist. Respecting people from around the world and being internationalist in orientation, the kinds of values I grew up with, were common in my family.

You might say I was confused about what class I belonged to. My privileged status suggested I was rich, but my father had debts to pay off because we lived in a Frank Lloyd Wright house, so he didn't think of us as rich. According to him, my three brothers and I were middle-class kids with a rich grandfather. But once my grandfather died, it was his inheritance that paid for our educations. My mother came from a working-class background in New York.

Jewish Culture

Did the Jewish culture of the family play any role in your upbringing?

Sure. We didn't eat pork, bacon, ham or catfish. I was bar-mitzvahed at the age of thirteen. I was also confirmed, though I can't remember at what age. I went to Sunday school, where my father actually taught, even if he was an atheist. There was a period when I was very young when I was quite religious, very much under the influence of a rabbi named Rothstein, who wasn't at all popular with the congregation. He was controversial and eventually was forced out, but I very much admired him.

I describe the process through which I lost my religious beliefs in the first chapter of my first book, *Moving Places*. I talk about having a nightmare that disturbed me because it seemed to be anti-religious. Then I spoke to my father and learned for the first time that he was an atheist, which shocked me at first, but then came to influence me.

Stanley Rosenbaum

Where was your father educated?

He went to Harvard, and then spent one year in graduate school in Denver, which is where my grandfather's two brothers both lived. But by this time—during the Depression—he couldn't find a teaching job, so he wound up working for his father at the Alabama theaters as a kind of default. It was not what he would have chosen to do himself, but what he wound up doing for maybe as much as three decades… For a considerable length of time, in any case.

I've often observed that the only real movie buffs in the family were my grandfather and me. My grandfather wasn't a buff in any esoteric way; I just mean he enjoyed movies a lot. He especially loved musicals. And even though my brothers went to a lot of movies, as I did, they didn't wind up as cinephiles.

When you became a film critic, did it encourage your father to share his memories of working in your grandfather's chain of cinemas?

We did talk about it, especially when I was writing *Moving Places*, but when I was growing up, I thought of myself as a literary writer. I wound up becoming a film critic, but it wasn't something I was thinking of doing when I was very young. Ever since I was in grammar school, I knew I was going to be a writer. I sold a one-page story to *The Magazine of Fantasy and Science Fiction* which I wrote when I was thirteen; it was published when I was fourteen. And then, around the same period, I won first prize for the best poem in a magazine called *Junior Scholastic*. So I had those early successes, and I was encouraged to write by my parents.

My father wrote a column in the local newspaper about the movies at Rosenbaum theaters that were playing in town that week. It obviously was advertising, but for him it was also an opportunity to give information and sometimes add personal comments. When he wrote about *The Eddy Duchin Story*, he mentioned going to hear Duchin play in Central Park when he was living for about a year in New York. If I was asked when I was ten years old what a film critic was, I thought then that would be what my father did: writing for the local paper rather than writing promotional ads for the movies he was showing. He once even invited me to take over his column for one week.

Do you remember which films you wrote about?

There were several, but the one I remember now is a Disney cartoon short that I'd already seen on a family trip called *Toot, Whistle, Plunk and Boom*. I said it was the best cartoon I'd ever seen!

Mildred Rosenbaum

What about your mother?

My mother was a New Yorker, and my father met her during his year in New York. She wasn't a movie buff and she certainly didn't care for cartoons. Two things ruled her existence. One was that she had been a very successful Powers model. To give you an idea of what a Powers model was, Grace Kelly played one of them in *Rear Window*. Mimi[*] was flown across the United States to do modeling work, as a poster girl for cigarettes and other products. She was one of the first women to wear contact lenses. And she was also very much involved in music. She'd studied music at Hunter College in New York and played the piano. I have fond memories of hearing her play when I was

---

[*] Mimi is what Mildred Rosenbaum's children called her.

young, and the first times I heard Stravinsky and Bartók was when she played them on records. But fairly early on, she lost confidence or interest in being a musician and stopped playing the piano, around the same time that I started playing myself.

Before marrying my mother, my father had a couple of serious romances with non-Jewish women that my grandfather had managed to break up, and my father was very resentful about this. Later on, my grandfather paid for him to go to New York with the idea that he was going to write a book and spend a year doing research for it. My mother's maiden name was Bookholtz, and there was a family joke that my father went to New York to write a book but came home with a Bookholtz instead. Originally he was interested in my mother's older sister, whose married name was Toby Lelyveld. She eventually became the mother of Joseph Lelyveld, who much later became the executive editor of *The New York Times*.

Toby herself became a published author. Her book, which grew out of her doctoral thesis, is about different interpretations of Shylock in *The Merchant of Venice*. It's an overview of attitudes towards Jews in different historical periods.* In any case, she already had a boyfriend and later husband, who was a rabbi. So at a certain point my father became interested in Mimi, one of her two sisters. My grandfather was so glad that Stanley, my father, was marrying a Jewish woman that he helped to finance the building of their house across the street from his own.

The Siblings

You had three siblings?

That's right. I was the second oldest. My older brother David was a real jock who became a lawyer and who, I'm sorry to say, committed suicide, shot himself, when he was in his forties. He was very much involved in sports, especially golf, and hit a hole in one when he was very young, which led to him being nicknamed Ace. He was very popular, whereas I was anything but. He had all the girlfriends; I usually didn't have any. He even dated the girlfriend I had a crush on, although I never told him that. In other words, we were seen and perceived ourselves as being the opposites of each other. There was one thing that sort of affected all of

---

* Toby Bookholtz Lelyveld's book was published as *Shylock on the Stage* (1960).

us—my three brothers and me—while we were growing up, and that's what I would call Jewish sibling rivalry.

This sort of stuff was probably made worse by my mother having grown up in a very competitive household with her sisters. I think she tended to compare each of her sons to the others, and we were encouraged to be rivals for her attention, as well as for my father's attention. It's one of the things that hung over me. What was so important about my relationship with my younger brother, Alvin, was that we were able to overcome all our sibling rivalry. We had to struggle against it in order to succeed, and then we became close in a lot of ways. Alvin and I went to the same college, for example. There were at least a couple of occasions where we were involved with the same woman. His former girlfriend became a girlfriend of mine or vice versa.

David, my older brother, and I grew up hating each other and fighting all the time. It was so serious that at one point, on a family trip to New York, we were taken to see a psychologist who, by the way, was Dr. Spock. Benjamin Spock wrote the most popular books about how to raise your children. I don't recall this meeting, but I was told his conclusion was that David and I would grow out of our rivalry, which turned out to be absolutely true. We got along fine when we were adults and less dependent on the approval or disapproval of our parents.

Our youngest brother, Michael, was neglected.* Well, I could say that *all* of us were in some ways neglected by our parents, and we were partly raised by black servants. But Michael largely grew up with our grandparents in Florence, and for him they played a parental role more than my parents did.

My father was very generous towards my brothers and me. We had something called Surprise Night. He worked at the theaters every night except Tuesdays and Thursdays. It was called Surprise Night because he would buy candy or popcorn to give us, which was the surprise, and then he would read to us. A lot of my introduction to literature was being read to, everything from *Huckleberry Finn* to *The Glass Menagerie* to *The Martian Chronicles* to *The Night of the Hunter*, the Davis Grubb novel. Novels, short stories, plays. Whatever he liked and wanted to share with us. Some

---

* Michael is the only one of Jonathan's siblings I have met. He was living in Islington, London, where he was a supporter of the local Member of Parliament Jeremy Corbyn, who at the time was leader of the Labour Party. I interviewed him for Mehrnaz Saeed-Vafa's documentary *A House is Not a Home: Wright or Wrong*.

of my favorite writers are those I first experienced when my father read them aloud to us.

In Mehrnaz Saeed-Vafa's documentary A House is Not a Home: Wright or Wrong, *I get the impression of a family that gradually grew dysfunctional.*

Well, my mother had lifelong mental problems; she was in therapy a lot. When we had family meals together, she would sit at the end of the table, not say anything, and leave early, or she wouldn't join us at all. She'd have her food brought to her in her bedroom. She really wasn't equipped to be a mother. And given the sexism of both Judaism and the South, she was expected to be beautiful and not have a brain. It was my father who was supposed to be smart. She was just supposed to be attractive. She was very much beloved in the community as a hostess, but for us, her children, she wasn't around much, and when she was there, she gave us a hard time about keeping the house presentable for visitors. She saw the house as an extension of herself, and was too narcissistic to care much about her kids except as a reflection of who she was.

She went away to a mental institution in New York in 1954 and stayed there for almost a year. In *Moving Places* I reproduced some of the exchanges we had, postcards and letters, during that period. On the other hand, my father had grown up as an only child and was very desperate to have kids of his own, and to have more than one so that they wouldn't grow up feeling lonely as he did during his own childhood. At the same time, he spent most of his free time in his study reading. An extra wing was designed by Wright to add to the house when the family got larger, and it was very important to build an almost soundproofed playroom that was also a bedroom, to cut off the kids from the rest of the house, which is where my parents were. This led to our largely being raised by black servants.

Babysat by Cinema

Still, to me, it sounds like an ideal situation because, on one hand, you had access to your father's library, and on the other, you had access to your grandfather's network of cinemas.

And not only that, but at the time, at least during my earliest years, there were three Rosenbaum theaters in downtown

Florence, all of them located within the same two- or three-block radius, making it very easy to walk from one to the other, and I'm sure my parents must have considered the movie theaters as a convenient kind of substitute for babysitting.

There's one item that I saw when I was very young, a movie in which poisoned biscuits played some role, that made me refuse an offer of a biscuit in a restaurant. I've been trying for most of my life to recover what film this was and to see it again. It was a great source of hilarity for my parents. It would have been a perfect film to write about in *Moving Places* if I'd been able to come up with the title of the film and what age I was at the time.

Do you remember much about the films you watched in your grandfather's cinemas during your early days in Florence?

Absolutely. To this day I still do have vivid memories of many of the films that I saw then. My favorite when I was seven years old was *Annie Get Your Gun*, which I saw many, many times. It's kind of significant to me because even though I love musicals, there was also a certain way in which I could identify with a young girl who dressed like a boy and behaved like a boy. In other words, a certain flexibility in relationship to gender was already meaningful to me. I remember even thinking as a young child that I wished I'd been a girl because girls weren't required or expected to go out and play baseball; they could stay at home. And I liked that. I also wished I'd had a sister, that I could have grown up with one. *Annie Get Your Gun* was definitely my favorite, and I even went to see it when it played across the river at another Rosenbaum theater.

And Delmer Daves' Bird of Paradise, *too?*

I saw that at the Princess in Florence. It was a traumatizing experience. Most of the strong memories that meant something are included in *Moving Places*.

Was there any kind of age restriction on the films you could watch in Florence?

There might have been for other people, but I had free reign of the theaters, although there were certain films that my father didn't want me to see because he thought I would be disturbed by them. That happened one day when he was going away on a trip for a day during which a film called *Freaks* was playing at the Majestic Theater. He said I definitely shouldn't go because I would find it upsetting. And then, naturally, I had to go because I was so curious. So I went to see it, and sure enough, I really got upset. Consequently, I wasn't allowed to see *The Thing From Another World* because my father decided that would be too disturbing to me. And also the very popular Andre De Toth horror film *House of Wax* in 3-D I wasn't allowed to see either.

I should mention something about the Jim Crow laws. The box office of the Shoals Theatre had two windows. The one in front was for the white patrons, the other one for black customers was around the corner on the side, with a side entrance that led up to the balcony. The prices for black people were cheaper. Black people had to pay less money to see them because they had less money. And when theaters became integrated by law, they kept the same prices and the same windows open, which meant that any white person who wanted to sit in the balcony for less money could, and any black person who wanted to pay more money and sit downstairs could. But, by and large, that didn't happen very often. That was how they were able to keep a kind of legal segregation going, at least in some theaters in the South, after the Civil Rights Act was passed. When I went back, I always sat in the black section.

Designed by Frank Lloyd Wright

You were raised in a house designed by Frank Lloyd Wright.

I used to say as a joke that the down payment on it was a gift to my father from his father for not marrying a shiksa—the Yiddish term for a non-Jew, usually a Christian.

My parents were not originally particular fans of Frank Lloyd Wright. They were friends with one of his students at Wright's Taliesen Fellowship, and originally they went to this friend with the idea of him designing the house. But the friend, a guy named Aaron Green, said, "Well, why don't you go to Wright himself? He could do a better job." Wright agreed to do it, although he never came to Alabama; he designed it all from Wisconsin or Arizona, which is where his own two homes were, and sent down some of his fellowship students to supervise the work.

The house was considered a real freakish thing in the community back then, although of course now it's a tourist attraction. The two leading tourist attractions in Florence today are the birthplace of W.C. Handy, the black man who composed "St. Louis Blues," a simple log cabin, and the fancy Rosenbaum house designed by Wright, which is now owned by the city.*

What's very strange is that today—as a museum—the books on the shelves of the Rosenbaum House are books that had belonged to me or my father or one of my brothers. I once wanted to take one of the books back with me after visiting there, and they said, "Okay, you can take this one, but you can't take any more," which is kind of crazy because the books are just there for décor.

We are all shaped by the spaces in which we grew up or the spaces in which we live. How did growing up in that house influence your character?

I'll give you one example: I don't have my shoes on now. I generally go around when I'm at home without my shoes, and this comes from growing up in a house which may have been one of the first, or maybe even the first, American houses to have heating through the floors. There were pipes under the floors, so that in the winter, if we wanted to keep warm, it was better to have our shoes off.

There were other ways in which I appreciated the house as a work of art, such as the way some of the rooms flow into each other. There are also steps going up or down at different parts of the house because Wright didn't believe in altering the terrain. So basically the house was built without any landscaping.

Wright was a great believer in privacy and private space, so the whole back of the house is glass doors facing the Tennessee River, and the front of the house is just cypress wood, with very high transoms. In other words, the house was and is closed to the public, whereas the back —a large backyard devoted to privacy—was more open but even more cut off from the community, like a fortress. I remember as a kid being envious of friends who had front porches because I loved the idea of saying hello to people as they walked by.

There was a reclusive aspect to the house that the older I get, the more I tend to criticize. Even though I got along with kids in my grammar school class, I tended to be very much a loner as I was growing up, enough of one that in my early teens, on Saturday afternoons, I'd go into my father's office, right next to the largest of the theaters, the Shoals, and write short stories on the typewriters.

---

* For more on the house, see https://www.wrightinalabama.com/.

Did that reclusiveness worry your parents?

My mother thought I should see a psychiatrist in Birmingham, and because she was already driving to see a therapist there on her own every Saturday, she insisted that I go and see a psychiatrist there also. It was absurd because he wasn't even a good psychiatrist; our sessions consisted of me describing and analyzing the dreams I'd had. I'd already learned enough about Freud to interpret them myself. Then I'd say to the psychiatrist, "What do you think?" and he'd reply, "That doesn't matter, Jonny. What's important is: what do *you* think?" And he'd never say anything else. So it was a total waste of time and money. I always thought that the stories I wrote in my father's office were a better form of therapy.

Early Education

What about your schooling?

It was during a conversation with my mother on the ride back from Birmingham that we came up with the idea of me going to a progressive boarding school where I could find people who shared my interests. A good friend of my family named Morris Mitchell had started a graduate school for teachers right next to the Putney School in Vermont, and we'd once paid him a visit, so we knew about Putney.

Once a year, Morris Mitchell would go on car trips with his grad students, and he always included Florence, where he'd previously lived and taught, in his travels. The Rosenbaum house was part of his itinerary, and I remember how fascinated I was by the national and ethnic diversity of his students. So there were indications of a much wider social universe that I encountered through these graduate students.

This was basically what led to me going away when I was 16 to Putney. Actually, I'd tried to go there the previous year but was too late in applying, so I wound up going there as a high school junior in 1959.

Did you return to Florence after the boarding school?

No, aside from summers and some school holidays. Right after I graduated from Putney in 1961, I decided to attend a radical summer camp in Monteagle, Tennessee, held at the Highlander Folk School. I wanted to go to the camp because I'd grown up in Alabama, where the only black people I'd gotten to know were a few cooks and babysitters. The idea was that the camp would be evenly integrated between white and black people. They couldn't get that many white people in the South to go, so in fact it was two-thirds black. The tent I was in had, I think, ten boys, and there was only one other white person. Being part of a racial minority was quite a learning experience, one that actually made it emotionally impossible for me to conceive going back to Florence, Alabama to live. I can still remember how different downtown Florence looked on a Saturday afternoon, the same day that I returned from Highlander. I was asking myself, "Why are there so many Negroes in town today?" until I suddenly realized that I hadn't really seen them before. It was a rude eye-opener.

This was the summer after I graduated Putney. I started college at New York University, and three semesters later transferred to Bard College, two hours' away by train or car. I missed being part of a community, and after visiting a former Putney classmate who attended Bard, a young black woman from North Carolina named Helen Quigless, I decided that the Bard community was the one I wanted to join. I was an English major.

So you could basically say I lived in Florence for the first sixteen years of my life, and afterwards I usually returned only during holidays.

Racism

Your brother Michael told me of an episode in Florence in which the Ku Klux Klan set a cross on fire in front of your house.

That happened long after I had left. Michael had been involved in a civil rights march, I think in Mississippi, and when interviewed by one of the news services mentioned that he was the son of a teacher at Florence State College, which my father was at that time, because the movie theaters were sold by my grandfather in 1960 during my senior year at Putney.

Somebody showed the news story to George Wallace, who was then governor of Alabama, and he actually ordered the president of FSC to fire my father. The president, to his credit, refused to do this. He could have gotten fired, but then there was the risk of FSC losing its accreditation. And even though the burning cross might have been only a prank of Michael's teenage classmates rather than the actual Ku Klux Klan, it did have the effect of making our father less outspoken about controversial subjects. Partly because of that Frank Lloyd Wright house, moving elsewhere wasn't really an option for him and Mimi.

There are clichéd ideas about racism in the South that sometimes overlook significant details. My favorite example of this is a childhood memory of W.C. Handy, specifically a visit to Florence that I only heard about later. He returned to town and gave a lecture at my one of my grandfather's theaters, the Princess. He was the son of a black minister, and remembered, around the turn of the century, that his father and a white minister would exchange congregations once a month. That, of course, blows people's minds because they think that could never have been possible in the segregated South. But it did happen, and apparently it wasn't even controversial. I'm not trying to soft-pedal Southern racism; I just want to cite a fact that doesn't fit the stereotypes.

You were critical of films like Mississippi Burning *about the inaccuracies in their portrayal of the racial tensions in the South.*

Especially the treatment of the FBI, because the people in the FBI were treated by that film as the heroes of the civil rights movement, which is an outrageous and disgusting distortion. At Highlander, when we were attacked or threatened, we already knew that the FBI wouldn't help us because they were on the side of the attackers. J. Edgar Hoover was himself a racist. He basically made every attempt to hound Martin Luther King to his death and even to try to get him to commit suicide by spying on him and then exposing his adultery.

Are there any frank and authentic films made about the South during that period that you can think of?

One I always cite as being the film that captures the South and Alabama better than any other film is *The Phenix City Story*, a powerful Phil Karlson thriller and docudrama. I especially like the way it uses a lot of local people. There was a progressive candidate for attorney general of Alabama who was assassinated, and that's what the movie is about: how this local lawyer was killed by the mob in Phenix City.

Another film worthy of mention, which I regard as Elia Kazan's best film, is *Wild River*, set in the same general area where I grew up. In his films *Baby Doll* and *A Face in the Crowd*, as well as *Wild River*, Kazan actually took pains to reproduce regional Southern accents accurately, and even hired a consultant. By the way, Kazan knew about Highlander Folk School, and so did Nicholas Ray. When I met Ray and told him I'd been to Highlander, his eyes lit up and he said, "Oh, wow! You know those people?"

The Birth of a Cinephile

When did you start to feel that you were hooked on cinema and that it was becoming a way of life for you?

During the time I was at Putney, I would spend occasional weekends in New York, as well as certain holidays because my mother's parents lived there and I also had cousins from there. This was the period when I saw *Hiroshima mon amour*, *Shadows*, *Breathless*, *Vivre sa vie* and The Living Theatre's original stage production of *The Connection*, which I saw three times.

When I was a freshman at NYU, there was a film club called Cinema 16, and I joined that as a member. The two films I saw there were Bresson's *Pickpocket* and Rivette's first feature, *Paris Belongs to Us*. So basically, being exposed to film as an art form was something that really only happened after I left Alabama, although I do remember a 1950 trip to New York, when I was seven, and seeing *City Lights* with my parents at the Museum of Modern Art. I even remember the animated Norman McLaren short with it, which used jazz, *Begone Dull Care*.

So there were a few indications of films that could be seen as art before I went to Putney, where I saw 16mm prints of *Citizen Kane* and *Alexander Nevsky*. *Kane* totally blew me away. Like many people, that was the beginning of my appreciation of film as an art form. I was about 17.

Heinrich Blücher

During the college years, were there any teachers or lecturers who made an impression on you and shaped your intellectual life?

Above all, the person who had an impact on me and was really the best teacher I ever had was Heinrich Blücher, a German teacher who was the husband of Hannah Arendt. One of her best books, *On Totalitarianism*, is dedicated to him. He never published a word in his entire life, but he influenced her, and she influenced him. He was very open, even back then, about the fact that Hannah Arendt had had an affair with Heidegger when she was his student, and that she went back to Germany to have a kind of reunion with Heidegger, despite the fact that he'd become a Nazi. In other words, that was an issue they had to deal with.

Blücher was amazing. I took two seminars with him. The first was called "Metaphysical Concepts of History and their Manifestations in Political Reality." The second seminar I took with him was on nihilism.

The first piece in *In Dreams Begins Responsibilities* is a piece I wrote for the Bard college newspaper, a review of *Dr. Strangelove*, which Blücher read and told me he liked. I even mention in the introduction how that piece itself was influenced by him. The dialectical way it was organized had an awful lot to do with his method. When I also wrote about the last legs of the Selma to Montgomery march for the *Bard Observer*, Blücher told me he liked that as well.

What was his teaching like?

What he would do was give these impromptu lectures about each of the figures we were studying—Hegel or Marx or Nietzsche, for example. He would first begin the lecture by saying everything that was praiseworthy about them, and then he would tear them to pieces. That was the manifestation of these metaphysical concepts in political reality.

When I look back at it now, I had some pretty good teachers, but I can't say that there were any that were profound influences, apart from Blücher. Another role model of mine at the time was Susan Sontag, whom I invited to Bard shortly before she became famous, specifically after she published "Notes on 'Camp'" but before it was discussed in the mainstream press.

Did you take any courses on aesthetics and arts?

I took one art history course. My favorite painter is Bruegel, and I took a course called "From Bosch to Bruegel," taught by a German art historian. But in terms of an actual course in aesthetics, no. There weren't any offered, as far as I can recall.

Aside from jazz, is it a coincidence that most of your early influences are from Central Europe?

It's funny that you mention that, because of my grandfather coming from Poland. But I think that there are certain common points between Eastern Europe and Iran, even a certain type of sense of humor, a certain way of being ironic about things.

So, yes, I'm sure that has played a role in my formation, but it would be hard for me to spell it out precisely, except to say that it's something that I'm very much aware of, even to the point of having written more than once about the fact that the filmmakers who were considered key leftist figureheads in the West were people like Godard and Antonioni, not filmmakers from Eastern Europe, even though aesthetically and politically figures like Miklós Jancsó, Věra Chytilová and Dušan Makavejev were actually the real radicals. I've come to appreciate them more over the years. I think part of the problem in the West was that we didn't have a cultural context for Eastern Europe; the Cold War made that impossible. We didn't know enough about those countries to be able to judge or even to situate them, which is why there tended to be this preference for French and Italian filmmakers, just because we knew a little bit more about the countries. There was so much propaganda, although paradoxically, American culture was more internationally oriented during the Cold War than it is now.

Why is America more culturally introverted today?

I'm not sure. You would think that the Internet coming along would put us more in touch with the rest of the world. It can probably be accounted for in part by economic interests and territorial markets. One way you can chart this is to note that Russian stereotypes in American cinema can be traced back to the '50s. A filmmaker wanting to signal to an audience that a character was from Russia would show someone angry, taking off his shoe, and pounding it on the table, which is what Khrushchev once did. The fact that they had to go back to the 1950s suggests that there weren't enough images of Russia since then that were recognizable to audiences. But it's hard to understand why there was more cultural interaction during the Cold War than there is today.

Jazz

How did you discover jazz?

One of my New York cousins while I was growing up, David Lelyveld, was a big fan of bebop and the Lennie Tristano school, especially Warne Marsh, and introduced me to those figures. On my own I had already discovered many others, including Dave Brubeck, Ahmad Jamal, Miles Davis

—specifically, his *Round Midnight* LP—the Modern Jazz Quartet and Stan Kenton. On February 22, 1957, five days before my fourteenth birthday, I went with my girlfriend at the time, Jean McIntosh, to hear a Louis Armstrong concert at the Sheffield Community Center, across the river from Florence. We went to the early show for whites only, not the 9:30 show for "colored" only, although it's worth adding that Louis Armstrong played with his white drummer, Barrett Deems, at both concerts, someone whom I wouldn't see perform live again for almost another forty years, when my friend Mehrnaz Saeed-Vafa and I caught him one New Year's Eve in Chicago, shortly before his death.

I should add that my mother had a minor interest in jazz, and she once went to the trouble of getting me a few lessons from a local piano teacher who knew a little bit about jazz, taught me a few chords, and even gave me a couple of his old albums that he no longer listened to: Billy Taylor with Candido and the Oscar Peterson Trio. I don't remember which album. I also played clarinet in my high school band and participated in a few local jam sessions. The usual drummer was the late Donnie Fritts, who years later became a composer and was a pianist for Kris Kristofferson.

Later, after I started college at New York University, I got to see a lot of stuff live, notably Charles Mingus, Bud Powell and Chico Hamilton at Birdland, Miles Davis at the Jazz Gallery. I can recall one stupendous weekday evening —when I got in for only $1, a student discount price—Miles was playing with John Coltrane, Cannonball Adderley, J.J. Johnson, Bill Evans, Paul Chambers and Philly Joe Jones. And believe it or not, the Teddy Wilson Trio was playing alternate sets! I also saw Miles and Mingus, and Bill Evans with Scott LaFaro at the Village Vanguard, Roland Kirk and Thelonious Monk and Ornette Coleman at the Five Spot, and Coltrane's classic quartet as well as Tristano with Marsh and Lee Konitz at the Half Note, Kenny Dorham and Roland Kirk at Slug's, and Archie Shepp at some long-gone hangout a block from NYU. I also saw Martial Solal and Billy Taylor on separate occasions at the Hickory House, but this was probably some years later. Actually, I went to see Mingus at many clubs, with many separate groups, and one of my fondest memories from that period was going up to him at many of those dates and requesting that he play "Peggy's Blue Skylight," which he always did.

After three semesters at NYU, I transferred to upstate Bard College, where I learned some more piano chords from a few classmates, played in a few jam sessions—at which Chevy Chase played drums, and I once also accompanied

Blythe Danner when she sang *Round Midnight* at a club on campus—and heard more live jazz in New York during weekends. I produced one concert at Bard myself, hiring Herbie Hancock, Ron Carter and Tony Williams. I also helped to promote another one that was produced by Chevy and Blythe, performed by the Bill Evans Trio.

Incidentally, during my five years in Paris, for a brief period I was friendly with avant-garde alto sax player Noah Howard and did an interview with him that I sent to *Downbeat*. They didn't publish it, but the editor, Don Morgenstern, wrote me back, encouraging me to submit more pieces, which I never did.

When did you sit behind a piano for the first time? Was it in Florence?

Yes. We had a grand piano in our living room, which is still there, although it's been out of tune for years. My mother played it. And at a certain point, what's really interesting is she stopped playing it, so maybe what's happened to me recently is another version of what happened to her. She became too self-conscious about it. In fact, I started playing that piano around the time that she stopped, although I was never anything more than an amateur jazz pianist whereas she was much more accomplished and played only classical music.

When I was still at NYU as a freshman in the early Sixties, I was sharing an apartment with two other guys who weren't even students, but there was a piano in my room, and I actually played it. I even wrote a few tunes, one of which I can be seen playing in Mehrnaz Saeed-Vafa's film *A House is Not a Home*, about the house I grew up in. Before that, there's a little bit of me playing the piano in a student film by Peter Bull in which I starred called *The Two-Backed Beast, or The Critic Makes the Film* (1978). In that film, made as a graduation film in San Diego, I was invited to lecture on an imaginary film; in other words, to make up the film in my own head and lecture on it as if it existed. And then a couple of his classmates tried to make the film that I was describing, intercutting the results with my lectures.

Peter was and is a very good filmmaker. He produces educational films now for PBS and made a first-rate jazz film that I rewatched recently, *Steve Lacy: Lift the Bandstand* (1985). For almost an hour you see Lacy describe his career and play with his group, without any of the interruptions or voiceovers that mar most jazz documentaries.

When you imagined a film and described it on camera, were you actually thinking of a specific film?

I was thinking of both *PlayTime* and *Out 1: Spectre*, an impossible fusion of two very different innovative French masterpieces.

Do you see any relation between your favorite jazz musicians and favorite film directors?

I've always thought that Mingus had a lot in common with Godard, especially in the way he incorporated both cultural history and the history of his own art, obliterating many of the distinctions we often make between modern and classical, or at least making most of them seem secondary. Also, I think both are political, polemical and stylistically eclectic in many comparable ways. They both have a genius for bringing together styles, forms and even topics that are generally believed to be incompatible. More indirectly, for their structured uses of silence, one could perhaps compare both Thelonious Monk and Ahmad Jamal to Yasujirō Ozu.

How do you think jazz has widened your scope?

A loose observation I can make linking jazz and film and writing for me, or what I like about all three: I'm preoccupied in a lot of my work with the coexistence of being alone in one's expressiveness and being part of a collective or a community, and discovering expressiveness that way. For me, much of the best jazz, film and writing grows out of a dialectic between these two kinds of expressiveness, as well as two kinds of response to that expressiveness.

Do you feel there is any affinity between playing an instrument and writing?

Yes. One of the things that I write about in my new collection is the performative aspects of criticism. What was so interesting about Manny Farber giving a lecture was that he was almost like a jazz musician improvising a solo. Jean-Pierre Gorin gave lectures like that also. On the Criterion DVD of *Pierrot le fou*, there's an audio commentary by him where he does something like "trade fours," exchanging four-bar passages of his own remarks with Jean-Paul Belmondo's voiceovers in the movie, giving it all a musical kind of delivery.

So, yes, writing is in some ways improvising. And I'm fascinated by the physical aspects of improvisation. I always love watching vibes players because you can't play that instrument without dancing. I even enjoy it when it comes out perverted and contorted, as in Keith Jarrett's moans and twisted postures, which I know irritate *you* sometimes. But I actually like how he throws his own body into his solos, even though you obviously can't go on doing that indefinitely, which may be why some fingers on one of his hands are paralyzed now. I think he screwed himself up by doing all that.

What I don't like about Jarrett's movements is that he does that but expects the audience to not move or make a sound. There was a joke about him complaining about the audience: "Now even the Japanese cough." I'm more in favor of Lionel Hampton. He dances, and wants to make the audience dance too. It becomes an interplay.

I see what you mean. Jarrett's behavior has always reminded me of some of the excesses of German Romanticism, which are also part of the Chet Baker cult, turning his sorrows into some version of Young Werner's. That's why *Let's Get Lost* irritates me, because the minute he starts playing, you almost immediately get a voiceover drowning out his solo.

Romanticism

What is your relationship with romanticism?

Very ambivalent and troubled. I regard myself in some ways as an artist, which gives me license to be self-indulgent about certain things. You have to be very good at what you're doing in order to justify that sort of entitlement. It's like you're increasing the stakes of whatever you're writing about. I address this problem in my essay about Fei Mu's *Spring in a Small Town*. Manny Farber once said something to me after I told him that I considered Preston Sturges' *Christmas in July* a Depression film, even though it was made after the Depression. "I'm not someone who ever survived the Depression," he said. "It's not something you ever get over." I feel that way about my adolescence. I never really survived or got over it. I'm still suffering. In that sense, romanticism is very much bound up in the attitudes one had as a teenager.

**NEW YORK
AND THE 1960s**

Let's go back to the transition from the 1950s to the '60s. When did you realize that you were in the 1960s, and that this was probably a new era for you and for America?

I guess it happened for me at Bard. The point is that the Beat Generation which was launched as an idea in the '50s sort of led into what became the counterculture of the '60s, the mainstream version. When I was at a boarding school in Vermont around 1960, I had my first experience with hallucinogens. Peyote was legal then. It was a few years later, in Manhattan and then at Bard, that I had my first experiences with marijuana. Both experiences were historical markers for me.

And of course, the civil rights movement was another factor that played a role, which also started in the '50s and blossomed in the '60s. I think almost everything that blossomed in the 1960s had begun in the '50s. Even the war in Vietnam—or what should maybe be called the war against Vietnam—was already an issue, at least in the world, if not in the U.S., in the 1950s.

Reading Criticism

When did you start reading film criticism and taking it seriously as a literary form?

I think it was around the time I attended Highlander, in the summer of 1961. I can remember going to the main office so I could read Dwight Macdonald's film columns in *Esquire*. He was the first contemporary film critic I became a big fan of. Actually, I'd met Macdonald at Putney because his son Nick was in the class below mine. Nick also became a film critic, and he's a good friend today. He wrote a very good book on his favorite film, *Grand Illusion*, and in some ways is more sophisticated as a film critic than his father was. I became aware of Macdonald's limitations as a film critic only much later. He began, when I started reading his column, with celebrations of the films that I was seeing and deeply impressed by, like *Hiroshima mon amour*, *Shadows*, *Breathless*, *L'avventura*, and *Last Year at Marienbad*. He ended up attacking *Muriel*, *Eclipse*, later Godard, and *2001: A Space Odyssey*.

Who else were you reading in the early '60s?

Probably Stanley Kauffmann. Raymond Durgnat's *Films and Feelings*, David Thomson's *Movie Man*, and several reviews and articles in *Sight and Sound*, by Tom Milne, Penelope Houston and others all had an impact. In *The New York Times* it was Bosley Crowther, who was such a bad critic that I even used him in a reverse way. If there was a film he was really offended by and disliked, I thought there was a good chance I would like it.

I bought my first issue of *Sight and Sound* when I was at NYU. That would have been around 1961 or '62. So I started reading film magazines, and that included fly-by-night magazines that came out in New York, like the *New York Film Bulletin*. The first time I read Andrew Sarris was probably in that journal. Jim Stoller's *Moviegoer*, which only lasted for three issues, was even better. There was *Film Culture*, of course, and during the early '60s, *Cahiers du Cinéma* came out for a little while in English. I still have those twelve issues. And I also read some stuff in French, with difficulty.

Did you also catch up with writers from the previous generation of American film criticism, like James Agee and Otis Ferguson?

Agee was the first collected critic, in terms of publishing all of his criticism in a book. I read him when I was at Putney because I was already interested in Agee as a Southerner and a literary writer.

Back then, I didn't know who Ferguson was. Even today, he's a critic I've never found to be very interesting, and it surprises me that people talk about him as being sharp and witty. I considered his taste philistine. What he had to say about jazz was not all that interesting to me either. As far as earlier American film critics go, I'm a big fan of Harry Alan Potamkin, who was a poet, a very interesting film critic, and a Marxist.* I guess he was also a communist. He went to Europe and interviewed Carl Dreyer and did all sorts of interesting things back in the 1920s.

What about Manny Farber?

I started reading him in *Film Culture*. My first impression was how peculiar he was. I began to appreciate him more as a writer and thinker over time.

---

* Harry Alan Potamkin (1900-1933). American critic who wrote for many publications, including *The New Masses*. A compilation of his work was published as *The Compound Cinema* in 1977.

Film Masters

Tell me about your earliest work as a film critic.

I still wasn't a film critic in my college days, except for an occasional piece, like writing about *Dr. Strangelove* for the Bard newspaper. I also ran a Friday night film series at Bard. What started me out as a film critic was somebody commissioning me to edit an anthology of film criticism, which I started working on when I was a grad student. That was around '67 or '68. It was a book that was going to be called *Film Masters*, and it twice went into galley proofs but was never published. But just by preparing the book, I became acquainted for the first time with people like Andrew Sarris.

The problem was that John Bragin, a friend who was at times a quite brilliant film critic himself, and who had all the stills and illustrations for the book, had become a Scientologist. After he got the advance on my book, he went off and worked on L. Ron Hubbard's fleet of ships, and became totally unreachable for the next two or three years. When I suddenly found that I couldn't bring out my book because I didn't have the stills, I had to fly back to New York, hire a lawyer, and go through all this rigmarole in order to have the rights to the book assigned only to me. Then it went into galley proofs, but they decided not to do it. The same thing happened with another publisher, who planned to do it and then changed their mind. It was a slow-motion torture that lasted for years, and although I still considered myself a novelist at this point, I couldn't find a publisher for either my second or third novels. I hadn't even tried to publish my first novel, written during my senior year at Putney.

I put a lot of time and effort into *Film Masters*. It would have been a good book, and it would have been a little bit in advance of what was going on then. I was very aware of French criticism. In fact, there were several translations that I commissioned of French texts, not just from *Cahiers du Cinéma* but other French sources, too.

Higher Education

Tell me more about your college years.

I spent five years as an undergraduate because certain credits from NYU didn't transfer and because I enjoyed

Bard so much. I also enjoyed programming my weekly film series, which helped launch my self-education in art cinema. Then I went to graduate school in English and American Literature at the University of New York at Stony Brook, mainly as a form of draft-dodging. I wound up looking for a good reason to quit graduate school after getting my master's degree the first year because I really hated it. I ended up doing everything except my dissertation, which was going to be about film and literature. I couldn't find a faculty member to referee my work. There was nobody who would take on my project about comparing literature and film.

Film Society

What can you tell me about the film society you ran at Bard?

A lot of the films I booked because I wanted to educate myself. They were films that I'd read about but hadn't been able to see. In fact, the only film course I ever took in my entire life, an "introduction to film" course at NYU, I took only because I wanted to see certain films. The first time I saw *The Birth of a Nation* and *The Last Laugh* was in that class. For the Friday night film series at Bard, I wrote little descriptions of the films in the campus newspaper. Some of those listings are on my website.

My favorite film at that time was *Sunrise*, which I'd seen on the Columbia University campus when I was at NYU. It was a film I actually showed twice at Bard because the first time I showed it, there were a lot of people hooting at it. They refused to take it seriously, and I was very upset by this. In fact, I can remember Stan Brakhage visiting the Bard campus because he was a big fan of one of the English teachers, Robert Kelly, who wrote poetry. When Brakhage came, he wanted to know if he could show as part of my series a short of his, the 26-minute *Prelude* to his *Dog Star Man*. I said, "Well, I'd be happy to show it, but only after we have shown the things that are scheduled for tonight because they are on the calendar, and people have come expecting to see them." And his attitude, although he didn't literally say it, was, "You're gonna show this Hollywood shit before my film?" That was then. Years later, not only was Brakhage quite reverential towards Murnau and *Sunrise*, he even gave lectures on Murnau that were very astute. But back then he was more embattled.

I can still remember the Q&A after his film. I actually tried to link his *Prelude* to *Sunrise* because of the use of superimpositions, for example. But again, he seemed irked by my saying that there was any way that I could compare his work to this Hollywood movie.

Incidentally, when I met Susan Sontag for the first time, at Bard, she won me over completely by describing how she'd wept when she saw *Sunrise*, which I believe must have been at the same Columbia University screening I had attended. At that point, she became my role model. Her passion was truly contagious.

By that time, were you fully aware that classical Hollywood was something to take seriously, and something which could be as artful as French and Italian cinema?

That was slow in coming, but it was already dawning. You have to remember that before Truffaut's book on Hitchcock came out, the whole idea of Hitchcock being an artist was very controversial in the States, whereas something like *Citizen Kane* and *Sunrise* being works of art—that wasn't a problem for me. But I wasn't there yet when it came to seeing Howard Hawks or Alfred Hitchcock or even Samuel Fuller as artists. I had taken Frank Tashlin seriously, from the time that I saw *Will Success Spoil Rock Hunter?* in Alabama, as a teenager. And I had been a Jerry Lewis fan too, but I don't know that I would've talked about Jerry Lewis as a serious artist.

The way cinema was generally regarded was so different then. During the 1950s, one usually went to movies just by going to a theater and walking in, not checking the times when the movie started. You just went in, and if it was the middle of the film, that was okay. You would stay until you reached this point where you'd come in, and then you left. Usually I would see films from the beginning, but I wouldn't consider it outrageous to see a film from the middle. The whole notion of spoilers came much later. It's a completely different mindset now.

Whenever my sisters and I wanted to watch films in foreign languages, we would first read a synopsis in a Persian film guide. Then, when we watched the film, we always knew in advance who the murderer was. It was more joyful and rewarding to watch films that way. It became about comparing our imagination of the story to the filmmaker's execution of it.

I understand. When I was writing about Yasuzo Masumura, there was a very gifted graduate student at the University of Chicago named Keiko Kinoshita, a former student of Shiguehiko Hasumi. She had a lot of Japanese videos of Masumura's films, and when she learned that I was interested in him, she did an amazing thing. She not only lent me the videos, she also wrote complete synopses of every scene and even listed the credits, so I could watch these films without subtitles. It's the same kind of thing that you and your sisters experienced. It was amazing that somebody would do something so generous. She's a very good critic and wrote her dissertation on Mizoguchi and Kinoya Tanaka, on the power struggles between them as reflected in the mise-en-scène of the films they worked on together. Portions of this have been published, not as a book, but as articles.

Do you subscribe to the notion that the 1960s were the golden age of cinephilia?

Up to a point. Discovering the art of cinema via French criticism and the French cinema informed by that criticism —Godard, Resnais and Truffaut—was a major worldwide event. But the discoveries of Asian, Middle Eastern and South American cinema that came later shouldn't be overlooked, and neither should the 1920s and early talkies.

When did you make your first festival trip as a film critic?

Let me think... I would say that when I was living in Paris, I went to Cannes three or four times and to San Sebastián once. But before that, when I was in graduate school and teaching freshman English, I wrote about the New York Film Festival and some of the films I saw there. So that started for me in the mid-'60s.

Drugs

Have you ever tried LSD? If so, have you ever written anything under its influence?

I took LSD at least three times, but I don't recall doing any writing on any of my trips. The first two times was with my youngest brother, Michael—once in New York and once in Paris—and on both occasions he abruptly abandoned me in media res, making the experience more depressing than enlightening, although on our second trip together we went to see Nicholas Ray's *Bitter Victory* at the Cinémathèque, which was a profound experience. My last acid trip, taken in Paris with a visiting woman friend from Alabama, was both exciting and blissful. We took a train to Chartres—the only time I've ever visited that cathedral—and stayed over at a nearby hotel… My first hallucinogenic experience, taking peyote in Putney during, I think, the spring of 1960, was also blissful. I think it permanently improved my appreciation of color, or at least brought me back to how I'd perceived colors as an infant, but I didn't do any writing on that trip either.

What else happened between the end of your postgraduate studies and your move to Europe?

I think it was during the mid-'60s, maybe towards the end of my period at Bard or just before I started graduate school, that I went to Paris for the first time. I really loved it. Then, during the summer of '68, I spent almost the entire summer there. I actually arrived the day the police took the Odéon back from the student activists. They were still repairing or replacing trees that had been uprooted on some of the boulevards and the cobblestones that were used to build barricades.

I was living in New York for most of the time I was in graduate school and commuting to Stony Brook in Long Island. I decided that I wanted to move to Paris. I often felt I was suffering from sensory overkill whenever I walked down streets in New York, and for me Paris offered a very pleasurable antidote to that, enhanced by my discovery of Jacques Tati's *PlayTime* in Paris, which taught me a different and poetic as well as humorous way of processing visual information.

PARIS

How did the move to Paris happen?

During the end of the summer of 1969, I rented a flat at 70 rue Mazarine, at the center of the Left Bank. The 6th arrondissement, very close to the Odéon metro station. I actually needed some help in doing this, and a friend who spoke French better than I did, Stephen Koch,* came to my rescue in working out all the details with the North African Jew I was renting from. I moved from New York to Paris in the fall of 1969.

    Part of what appealed to me about Paris was the literary mythology—Joyce, Hemingway, Fitzgerald, the writers and other artists who lived there. But it also had to do with the perception, which I still hold today, that the French know better, much better than Americans, how to enjoy themselves. I really felt that I could learn how to take more pleasure in life by living in Paris, and this is why, even today, I regard that city as my home more than Florence, Alabama. I moved there with no plans about when or if I would return to the U.S. In other words, it was very open-ended. These days, if I go to Florence, usually after two days I start to feel restless and uncomfortable.

Did you start going to the Cinémathèque right after your arrival?

I was going to all these cinemas on the Left Bank and the Cinémathèque, which actually had two different outlets, one of which was in the 5th arrondisement and one of which was on the other side of Paris. It was the one near the Eiffel Tower at the Palais de Chaillot that I went to most often. It was very cheap. Back then you could get into movies with a student card for one or two francs. It was almost nothing, literally a few pennies, to see a film.

Who were the critics you admired most when you were in Paris?

Apart from Lotte Eisner, who quickly became a friend—I used to visit her at her flat in Neuilly, where she liked to serve me Chinese tea—the two main influences I had, among other critics, during the period when I lived in Paris, were Andrew Sarris and Noël Burch. Burch is almost like the reverse of Sarris, so it was almost a dialectic. And back then,

---

* Stephen Koch (b.1941). American novelist, essayist, and teacher. His books include *Stargazer: Andy Warhol's World and His Films* (1986).

I was reading Noël Burch in French, although there had been a couple of his pieces published in English that I read. His *Praxis du Cinéma* hadn't yet been translated as *Theory of Film Practice*. That and Sarris' *The American Cinema* became my principal guides to what films I should see that I hadn't seen. I would even underline the titles in the books' indexes after I watched them. Though Noël Burch changed later, I think his formalism was a big influence on me. I was already interested in the Russian formalist critics when I was living in Paris. Another formative French text that I read in French at the time was Roland Barthes' *Le plaisir du texte*.

Odd Jobs

What was your source of income in Paris?

I inherited money from my grandfather when he died in 1962. Basically, he left money to my brothers and me, and that also paid for most of my education. There was enough money left over to support me during about half of the five years that I spent in Paris. It was only after that money ran out that I started looking, mostly unsuccessfully, for work. I wrote a draft of a screenplay for a producer and translated some treatments. I also subtitled a couple of films and landed a cushy job writing about films and interviewing Paul Morrissey for a monthly skin magazine called *Oui*. But it still wasn't enough to support me. I went through a period when I was literally if not broke, then very close to it. It's true that if I really got desperate, my family could bail me out. I would cook a curry that would last for a whole week. It was the only thing I would eat. I also sold some of my books in order to eat. The closest I've ever come to poverty was during the latter part of my period in Paris.

Which films did you subtitle?

The first one was Claude Lanzmann's first feature, *Pourquoi Israël*, which had been selected for the New York Film Festival. I didn't know who he was or anything about him then, and I wasn't that crazy about the film. The second one, which I barely remember now, was Liliane Dreyfus' *Femmes au soleil*, for the San Francisco Film Festival.

The first person I ever met in Paris was Bernard Eisenschitz. Somebody had given me his name and contact information, so he's my oldest Paris friend. He's only one year younger than me. I remember getting really angry with him once. I was puzzled by why there was so much reverence on the part of French writers, at least at the *Cahiers du Cinéma*, for Fritz Lang's *The Tiger of Eschnapur* and *The Indian Tomb*. When I asked Bernard about it, he said, "Oh, it's too complicated. You wouldn't understand." I was very offended. The funny thing is that in my new book, I include my own appreciation and defense of these films. Today, I not only understand why they liked them, but I share their attitude. It's this notion of being consciously naïve—deliberately becoming or at least pretending to be naïve when you're not naïve or innocent—that's part of what's unusual about those films.

Bernard had a kind of partnership in subtitling with a guy named Pierre Cottrell, who also produced Eric Rohmer's films and *The Mother and the Whore*. He and Eisenschitz together did a lot of subtitling work. Pierre took me on and gave me those jobs because I needed the work. It was his wife Edith who hired me to write a first draft screenplay. They were wonderful benefactors. At one point, after they got me a job translating a French film treatment into English, and the filmmaker in question refused to pay me, they paid me the fee themselves.

A Bresson Extra

How did you end up as an extra on the set of Robert Bresson's Four Nights of a Dreamer?

One night I was watching *Advise and Consent* at the Palais de Chaillot Cinémathèque. As I walked out, somebody came up to me and said, "Would you like to be an extra in a Robert Bresson film?" I said, "Sure." She said, "Well, we're shooting only a few blocks away." So I went with this person to where they were shooting, and then I called up my girlfriend, Connie Greenbaum, whom I was living with at the time, and invited her to join me. So both of us were extras. It was the next to last night of shooting.

A woman on the crew with whom I became friends was an Indian woman called Nasreen Munni Kabir.[*] I wonder if you know her since she also lives in London.

---

[*] Nasreen Munni Kabir (b.1950). Writer and documentary filmmaker specializing in Indian cinema. She programs Hindi films for Channel 4 in Britain and has authored numerous books, including one on Guru Dutt.

Yes, in fact I met her very recently, but not in London. We actually had lunch together in Mumbai.

She was a *stagiaire* on *Four Nights of a Dreamer*, and she told me about the next night's shooting, which was actually near Pont Neuf, very close to where Connie and I lived. It was the *bateau-mouche* sequence, the film's highpoint. They had already shot the film's two leads watching the boat, and this time they were filming the boat itself. I was there for the last two nights of the shooting. The first thing I ever published in *The Village Voice* was a piece about that experience called "Two Nights of an Extra: Working with Bresson." Not a very good piece. I went on to become friends with Munni. She then called herself Pakistani, and now she considers herself Indian, but I don't understand any of the complications and the nuances of that.

Which other filmmakers did you meet or observe working during your stay in Paris?

I watched Alain Resnais shoot *Stavisky* both in the studio and on location at a theater. I had arranged to interview Godard and Gorin about *Tout va bien*, but then they met me only to say that they couldn't do it because Godard was still recovering from his motorcycle accident.

I was commissioned by *Time Out* to interview Marco Ferreri, but that turned into a disaster. Ferreri hated me, and I wasn't that much of a fan of his. It was his film *La Grand Bouffe* that I was interviewing him about.

And of course I met Jacques Tati and Rivette. The point is that Paris is a very small world, so it becomes relatively easy to meet people. And, of course, there's also a story I like to tell about how I came to meet Orson Welles in Paris. Do you know that story?

Meeting Orson Welles

Tell me about it!

Basically it started with one of the first things that I wanted to write for *Film Comment*. I had a friend named Carlos Clarens.[*] He was a Cuban film critic and a protégé of Henri Langlois who later wrote very good books on horror films and gangster films. He also wrote for *Sight and Sound*.

---

[*] Carlos Clarens (1930–1987). Film historian and writer, chiefly known for his *An Illustrated History of the Horror Film* (1967).

Anyway, he had a copy of Welles' final draft of his script for *Heart of Darkness*. I was always fascinated by that project, and Welles' idea of using a first-person camera. I wanted to write an article about it. Someone said to me, "You should interview Welles about it. He's in Paris now, editing a film." I said, "He's not going to want to talk to me." At this point, I had published practically nothing.

I found out that Welles had a secretary based in London, so I called Mrs. Rogers long distance in London to ask about possibly interviewing Welles, and she said, "Look, why don't you write a letter and send it to him? He's very busy. Please don't call him and don't pester him. But you can write him a letter." She gave me the address of his editing studio, so I wrote him a letter and sent it off on a Saturday afternoon. Sunday night, I completed a whole draft of the *Heart of Darkness* piece, thinking I'm not going to hear from Welles anyway. I stayed up all night, and went to sleep around seven. Two hours later, my phone rang. The person on the line said, "This is an assistant of Orson Welles. Mr. Welles was wondering if you'd like to have lunch with him today." The lunch was at a restaurant within walking distance from where I lived, La Méditerranée, which is the same restaurant you see in *F for Fake*. The first thing I said to Welles was, "I'm amazed that you invited me to lunch." He said, "Well, I didn't have time to answer your letter."

One thing that this story illustrates is how efficient the Paris postal service was at the time. I would get three mail deliveries daily at rue Mazarine.

Private Screenings

Did you attend any private viewings of films?

I got to attend a lot of private screenings of Rivette's *Céline and Julie Go Boating*, because during the latter part of my time in Paris, my best friend, the Argentinian Eduardo de Gregorio, was Rivette's main screenwriter. He looked me up and we became sort of fellow cinephiles, so to speak.

There was a place called Club Thirteen—Club Treize—which was run by Claude Lelouch, a filmmaker I had no particular interest in. But it was a very nice place to have screenings, and every time I went to a screening of one of the work prints of *Céline and Julie Go Boating*, it was there. That's just one indication of how you keep running into all sorts of people. They weren't very hard to find or access.

I generally didn't go to press shows in Paris. I wasn't on that circuit. But I do remember seeing *F for Fake* for the first time at a press show with Lotte Eisner, because she invited me. I'll never forget that when the film was over, I said, "This isn't like most Welles films." She said, "It's not even a film."

Is your passion for Rivette partly rooted in the freedom his actors enjoy during the filmmaking process?

Not all actors enjoy the freedoms that Rivette sometimes bestowed on them. Years after I met Geraldine Chaplin in France during the shooting of *Noroît*, I ran into her at a film festival in Savannah and asked her what she thought of the film. She made it clear that she'd never seen it and had no interest in seeing it. I don't know if she felt that way about her other work for Rivette, but it clearly wasn't just fun and games for her, although she loved working with Altman on *Nashville* and told me so when I interviewed her about this in France. But I especially love the imaginative performances of Bulle Ogier in *L'amour fou* and Jean-Pierre Léaud in *Out 1*.

What can you tell me about the screenplay you wrote for Edith Cottrell?

It was an adaptation of a J.G. Ballard novel, *The Crystal World*. My first and only script. One of Edith's best friends was Jean Seberg, so the first person who read my script was Jean Seberg. She even invited me to her apartment to discuss it, and I spent an afternoon talking to her. She liked my script more than I did. It was alienated labor, and I was writing it because I needed the money. But it also led, indirectly, to a script conference with Susan Sontag. When I ran into Susan in Cannes and she asked what I was doing, I said I was writing a script based on a J.G. Ballard novel. She asked who was going to direct it. I said, "I don't know. We're looking for someone who might be interested." She said, "*I'm* interested!" So I had one meeting with her in her Paris flat about this lousy script.

That type of running into people happened a lot. It happens a lot in New York, but it happens even more in Paris because Paris is so snug and centralized. I mean, in the U.S., you've got Hollywood on one coast, and then on the opposite coast you've got the critics who have power. In the United States, the film world is split into two parts on opposite coasts, but in Paris, it's all in one place.

Jacques Tati

Did you get into any conversations with Jacques Tati at any point about writing something for him?

I was hired by him as a "script consultant," but I didn't even know what that meant and what he wanted, until it eventually became clear that he needed an audience whenever he was acting out a proposed sequence. Before that became clear, I tried to write a sequence on my own, something about a lot of TV sets in a shop window, because the film he had in mind, *Confusion*, was going to be about television. I quickly discovered that he wasn't even remotely interested in what I was doing because all his ideas came from either his own observation or his own brain and body. He did actually have a short treatment that had already been written and which at some point he showed me. But he never asked me to write anything.

How did he find out about you?

I had interviewed him for *Film Comment*. The reason that happened was because his assistant, a French-American woman named Marie-France Siegler, was from Birmingham, and at one point Tati came to the U.S. and visited Birmingham. My mother read about this in a local newspaper and managed to find out where Tati's office was, and thanks to her I was able to interview him. Later, Marie-France hired me to write the English screen narration for a short film that she had made called *The Last Night of Les Halles*, about the closing of Paris' fruit and vegetable market. Then she called me saying that Tati would like to work with me. Tati was very depressed at the time. He was bankrupt and wanted to get back to work, but it always helped if somebody else was around. He obviously liked me because of my enthusiasm for *PlayTime*. It was likely Marie-France's suggestion that he hire me.

So by the early 1970s, you had started writing professionally as a film critic. Were you also writing for Cahiers du Cinéma *at that time?*

No, it wasn't until years later when I was living in New York that I briefly became the New York correspondent for *Cahiers*, when Serge Daney was the editor. I even did interviews with Serge in New York, when we interviewed Brian De Palma and Alan Pakula, both for the "Made in USA" issue.

When I was living in Paris I did once write for *Positif*. Michel Ciment commissioned me to write about and interview Jim McBride. I knew McBride because my best friend in the States, Lorenzo Mans, was very close to him and wrote the script for his *Glen and Randa*. He also appears in *David Holtzman's Diary*.

Michel Ciment

*What did you think of the book of interviews with Michel Ciment—*A Shared Cinema?*

Cineaste, which sometimes invites critics to write letters commenting on pieces, asked me to write a letter about the excerpt from that book that they ran. My letter was mostly respectful, but honestly, I've always had mixed feelings about Michel. I see him as someone who had very conventional taste to the point of being sometimes quite naïve. What I objected to in the excerpt was that he said the worst thing a critic can do—I'm paraphrasing—is to criticize a film for its intentions. I said that it's naïve to think you can know anybody's, any artist's, intentions. That's a dangerous area to get into. But Michel never saw that as a danger. He just thought everybody has an intention when they make a film, and that's what we should consider. The whole thing strikes me as some kind of amateurish error.

On the whole, so much of his personality was dictated by this rivalry with *Cahiers du Cinéma* and finding negative things to say about them. He could write some very good critiques, and, of course, his interview books are among the very best interview books anybody has done—the ones with Kubrick and Losey especially.

He reviewed one of my collections. And some of the criticisms that he made of *Placing Movies* are ones I agree with. In that book, I included a bibliography of what I thought my best pieces were that weren't included in the book. He thought that was rather pretentious of me. He also took exception to me criticizing Donald Richie's book on Ozu for recycling phrases and statements that he'd made in his previous pieces, saying that's a completely normal thing to do and not worthy of criticism. Of course, I do it myself all the time now, so he was right to criticize me about that.

---

* I asked this question because Paul Cronin, the publisher of the book you are reading, sent us a copy of his English translation of the Michel Ciment interview book and invited us to embark on a similar project.

Michel definitely had certain virtues, but when it came to things like the avant-garde and experimental cinema, I thought he was a bit of a philistine, for example when he spoke about Béla Tarr being a very impressive filmmaker but "making a nine-hour movie is a bit much," or words to that effect. Of course, he was talking about *Sátántangó*, which is seven hours long. Temperamentally, I never felt that Michel and I belonged to the same tribe or group, even though I was surprised to discover recently that he was also Jewish.

André Hodeir

I have heard you refer often to another Frenchman—André Hodeir.

For me, Hodeir is something of a role model, especially in what he's taught me about form, and in some ways more as an artist than as a critic, especially his musical masterpiece *Anna Livia Plurabelle*. I love it when, as a critic, he compared Gil Evans' work transforming the compositions of others on *Miles Ahead* with the work of Jorge Luis Borges. More generally, I think he's had more to say and do regarding the interface between jazz and literature than anyone else. For instance, I'm fascinated by the fact that, even when he has his singers on *Anna Livia Plurabelle* mispronounce some of Joyce's puns, there always seems to be a good musical reason for doing so. The fact that this long work undergoes continual transformations is part of its power, even though not a single note is improvised. I do think it swings, however.

The High Screens of Paris

What else did you like about the film scene in Paris?

One thing that appealed to me about French cinemas is that they are constructed somewhat differently from American and English ones. It was one of the things that appealed to me about France. There's a certain kind of setup where the screen is higher so that the movie sort of falls on top of you. It seems to me that's very specific to French cinemas. It emphasizes the degree to which one becomes passive when confronted with the assault of a film.

LONDON

So you were down and out in Paris, and even slightly depressed. What happened after that? How did you end up moving to London in August 1974?

I had been writing with some regularity for *Sight and Sound*, starting with an article reviewing *Godard on Godard*, and the magazine's editor, Penelope Houston,* liked my stuff, even going to the trouble of hiring a lawyer to convince the government that this job should go to me, an American, and not to anybody else who applied for it. I was very moved by such a vote of confidence in my work. Even so, I would have happily stayed in Paris rather than move if it had been economically feasible, but I wasn't making enough money to pay my rent and expenses.

Where in London did you move to?

I took a sublet for about a month in St. John's Wood. I can't remember now how I wound up there. Then I moved to a maisonette on Branch Hill in Hampstead Heath, which I shared with a few other people, including Yehuda Safran, an Israeli lecturer in art who taught at Goldsmith College and whom I collaborated with on a review of Alexander Kluge's *Occasional Work of a Female Slave* for *Sight and Sound*. From there I moved to Belsize Park, where I stayed for much longer. Do you know Joel Finler?†

No.

He's an American who went to the London School of Economics, then stayed on in London. A film buff who wrote a book about *Greed* and collected film frames discarded by projectionists. He lived between Swiss Cottage and Belsize Park, and I rented a room from him. Then I moved again, this time to Chelsea, to share a flat with Tom Milne,‡ which is where I stayed the longest.

With all my books and records, it was difficult to move each time, and in some ways it was hard to adjust to London after Paris because the cities are so antithetical.

---

*Penelope Houston (1927-2015). British film critic and editor of *Sight and Sound* (1956-1990). Author of several books, including *The Contemporary Cinema* (1963).

† Joel Finler (b.1938). American film historian, resident in London since the 1960s. Author of *The Hollywood Story*.

‡ Tom Milne (1926-2005). British film critic. Associate editor of *Sight and Sound* and editor of the *Monthly Film Bulletin*. Editor and translator of *Godard on Godard* (1972).

Sight and Sound/Monthly Film Bulletin

What was your gig at Sight and Sound?

Being the assistant editor of *Monthly Film Bulletin* was the main part of my job. The second part was being a staff member at *Sight and Sound*. The two magazines had adjoining offices, with David Wilson, Penelope's deputy, stationed in between.

Were you at the Dean Street offices every day?

Yes. Richard Combs, the *Bulletin*'s editor, who hailed from New Zealand, and I singlehandedly put together every issue. Or at least we did until we eventually acquired a secretary to help with the typing—Sue Scott-Moncrieff, the niece of C.K. Scott-Moncrieff, the original English translator of Proust—and moved to a larger office space next door.

Richard and I assigned reviews to writers, mostly freelancers, and handled submissions, but there was an awful lot of work involved in just typing out all the credits for all the films. The stated mission of *Monthly Film Bulletin*, a publication slightly older than *Sight and Sound*, was to list the major credits and synopsize and review every feature film released in Britain and a selection of shorts. To get the credits, we'd often go downstairs to the BFI's Information Department and check the trade journals, and sometimes we also had to carry 35mm reels from distributors on Wardour Street to the BFI a block away on 81 Dean Street, then run the reels through a Steenbeck just to copy down the credits. Ironically, we had to do this most often for dubbed, continental, softcore porn films, which usually had credits that no one cared about. These generally had no pressbooks because their distributors wouldn't bother to gather any of this information. But we still had to get all this information and transcribe it, so we had quite a lot to keep us busy.

It was impressive that the whole issue could be put together each month by just the two of us. I remember once we had each issue done and ready to go, Penelope would come in to make a few comments and suggest changes. She had to approve whatever we had done, but it was always a relaxed and friendly atmosphere.

Many people considered the credits and synopses in the *Bulletin* to be objective, thereby supposedly justifying its state support, and the reviews to be subjective, but I believe this is misguided. Anyone who studies Hollywood knows that studio credits, which the *Bulletin* nearly always honored, are often inaccurate, and in my opinion there's no such thing as an "objective" synopsis. Alexander Walker* used to complain about what he regarded as the *Bulletin*'s leftist slant, which for him compromised its status as a state-supported publication.

Did you enjoy working for the British Film Institute?

Yes, I did, most of the time. The offices were all quite small, so it was a bit cramped, but that was something we quickly adjusted to. Penelope had a secretary of her own named Sylvia Loeb, who was quite a character—upper-class accent, very smart and intelligent, very right-wing, and also quite racist, with lots of opinions of her own, especially about classical music. Even though she was Jewish, she was both anti-Semitic and anti-black.

Did that job connect you with other writers in the English-speaking world, given that you were sometimes responsible for commissioning pieces?

Most of the commissioning was done by Richard Combs, except when he was away on holiday. But I was also doing some of it.

As a *Sight and Sound* staffer, I had occasional input in editorial matters, but mostly I was a contributor who had some say in what I contributed. I also managed to get certain things by other writers into *Sight and Sound*, such as reprinting Manny Farber's essay on Raoul Walsh when the National Film Theatre† was doing a Walsh retrospective.

Did you attempt to bring on additional French contributors due to your experiences in Paris?

Not really. There would have been a language barrier, because the French people wrote in French. And I didn't know that many. I mean, I knew some regulars at the Cinémathèque, but these were mainly American or English or from Latin America, and it was only much later that I formed many of my friendships with French film people.

What were your primary regular cinemas in London, aside from the NFT?

---

*Alexander Walker (1930-2003). British film critic. Resident at the London *Evening Standard* (1960-2003) and the author of many books.
† The National Film Theatre, now renamed BFI Southbank, is the public screening and cinema space of the British Film Institute.

I went to press shows, which were often on Wardour Street. I didn't go to cinemas often because I was already seeing so much. The BFI's location in Soho was very convenient because most of the distributors were close by. It was also a good neighborhood for restaurants; Penelope would take me to an excellent Italian place for occasional lunches.

There was a place on Dean Street, a block away from the BFI, called Royalty House, where periodically there would be a screening of something held by the National Film Archive. They sometimes also set up special screenings for staff or visiting film scholars. The first time I saw *The Great Garrick*, a wonderful James Whale comedy, was when Eduardo de Gregorio requested a screening as part of his research for a screenplay he was writing. He was fascinated by the notion of a "period" noir.

Are there any essays or specific issues of the magazine from the period that you are particularly proud of?

My first essay about the Edinburgh Film Festival, where I wrote about *Moses and Aaron*, *Rameau's Nephew by Diderot*, *Speaking Directly* and *Jeanne Dielman*.

When Richard was away on holiday, I put a still from Michael Snow's *Wavelength* on the *Bulletin*'s cover to illustrate my own review. That got me into *Private Eye*'s "Pseuds' Corner," and at least one *Bulletin* reader cancelled his subscription in protest. I also inaugurated the magazine's back cover feature with a Straub-Huillet bibliography.

As for my own longer pieces, I remember before I moved to London, there was a piece on *Lancelot du Lac* by Bresson that I worked on really hard. I saw the film twice with Bresson and his cast and crew in order to write the piece. The first issue that came out with a lead article by me, in fall 1974, carried my piece on *Out 1: Spectre* and *Céline and Julie Go Boating*, "Work and Play in the House of Fiction," which was probably the most ambitious and best piece I did for *Sight and Sound* up to that time. I was also proud of the fact that I managed to work in the names of all the two dozen lead actors in *Nashville* when I reviewed that film for *Sight and Sound*.

There were also many things I got assigned to do, such as short news stories for the "In the Picture" section and certain shorter reviews, including *Daisy Miller*, *The Tenant*, *The Godfather Part II*, *Nashville* and *Family Plot*. But I believe I was the one who instigated all my book reviews. And as I recall, Penelope assigned me to write briefly about the discovery of the preview version of Welles' *Touch of*

Evil, but I was the one who decided to report favourably in the same story on Stephen Heath's lengthy analysis in *Screen* of the release version.

London Film Festival

Were you also involved with the London Film Festival?

Oh, absolutely, at least as an audience member. One thing that was exciting for me about the London Film Festival was that I met people there that I never would have met otherwise, including, for the first time, after having seen and written about *Jeanne Dielman* at Edinburgh, Chantal Akerman. They had my review posted in the guest room, so the first thing she did before she even talked with me was go and read it. I watched her reacting to it point by point, which was interesting. She was glad that I mentioned the ceramic vase on the table where Jeanne Dielman puts all her money. She was really glad that I drew attention to that.

I also got to meet Marie Seton, the woman who wrote the first major Eisenstein biography in English, and Yuliya Solntseva, the widow of Alexander Dovzhenko, who played the lead part and title role in *Aelita*. Yuliya didn't speak any English and I didn't speak any Russian, so it was just saying hello to each other, but I was delighted nonetheless. Her 70mm film *The Enchanted Desna*, about Dovzhenko's childhood, based on his own script, was a particular favourite of Cinémathèque regulars, myself included, and I continue to love it even when I watch it on YouTube.

I remember meeting Robin Wood[*] for the first time at the London Film Festival. Of course, he was rather suspicious of me because he regarded *Sight and Sound* as the enemy. I also knew people at the BFI in other departments, like Jim Hillier.[†] And of course David Meeker,[‡] who had been the previous flatmate of Tom Milne before I moved in. Meeker was always sort of irascible and very opinionated, and always thought I was an asshole because I liked Jacques Rivette.

---

[*] Robin Wood (1931-2009). British film critic. Author of many books, including *Hitchcock's Films* (1965).
[†] Jim Hillier (1941-2014). At the BFI Education Department throughout the 1970s and editor of two translated collections of materials from *Cahiers du Cinéma*.
[‡] David Meeker (1935-2023). Film archivist. At the BFI from 1961. Author of *Jazz in the Movies* (1977).

David Meeker once told me he was proud that he had managed to block a Roberto Rossellini retrospective at the National Film Theatre.

David was impossible about these crazy ego games that he got into. Even if I would thank him for getting his help, he then would castigate me later for not thanking him. You probably had some of those same games with him. Incidentally, it was because of him that none of the BFI Classics has ever been devoted to a Rivette film, though I'm sure he was as dismissive of *Screen* as he was of Rivette. He made up the canon and established what books could or couldn't be done.*

You also mentioned the first Iranian film you saw was at the London Film Festival.

Yes, Parviz Kimiavi's *The Mongols*, which was a knockout. I also had an Iranian flatmate when I was living on Branch Hill, a woman named Mitra. It's amazing that around the same time Mehrnaz Saeed-Vafa and I were living in London and probably attending some of the same screenings at the NFT, but we didn't know each other. She was even friends with my flatmate, who worked as a dental assistant. An incredible coincidence!

Penelope Houston

Today, I believe that Sight and Sound *is far more international in its perspective compared to* Cahiers du Cinéma.

That's a legacy it owes to Penelope Houston. Maybe to Gavin Lambert also. In fact, Penelope has never gotten enough credit for wanting *Sight and Sound* to be an international film magazine. At least two-thirds of the pieces were written by people she never met, who submitted work without invitation. In other words, if there was something interesting going on in the world and it hadn't yet come to London, she was still interested. She didn't just want to service London audiences.

---

* Meeker aimed to curate a repertory of classic feature films for year-round screenings at the NFT. Initially focusing on a hundred titles, he expanded the list to 360, ensuring audiences had access to newly struck 35mm prints of seminal films. Meeker's selection was deeply personal, reflecting his own tastes. The initial commissions of the BFI Classics publishing series were drawn from his list.

I don't think she ever got any proper credit for her open-mindedness. She was seen as old-fashioned—correctly so in some ways, but incorrectly in others. She became a villain to so many people that her virtues are totally ignored, or at least they tend to be in the English film world. I would still argue that the best criticism I've ever read of *Last Year at Marienbad* is her review.

I remember one thing Penelope once said to me. It sounds immodest to report this, so I'm a little embarrassed about mentioning it, but she said that the best writers for her were the ones that required the least editing. And the only one she could compare me to in that way was Kenneth Tynan. She never was able to make many changes in his copy because what he wrote seemed perfect.

Penelope had a special interest in certain filmmakers, such as Preston Sturges and Stanley Kubrick and Nicholas Ray. *Sight and Sound* is credited with being the magazine that discovered Nicholas Ray, even before *Cahiers du Cinéma* did. And as you may know, Gavin Lambert and Nicholas Ray became lovers. Ray got him to leave England and his job as editor of *Sight and Sound* in order to join him in Hollywood and work on the script of *Bigger Than Life*. That's when Penelope took over as editor.

Did you have any encounters with Gavin Lambert?

I only met him once when he was back on a visit and was talking to Penelope in her office. He was very unfriendly to me. I'm still in the dark about why this was the case. I was eager to become friendly with him but he was eager for me not to be. Maybe he didn't like my long article about Nicholas Ray, but if that was the problem, I really don't understand what he would have objected to.

Sight and Sound Polls

I am curious how, for Sight and Sound's *poll of the best films of all time, you were able to bring on board such a diverse range of individuals, including those with opposing views.*

All I can say is that Penelope knew whom to write to and ask for a ten-best list. That feature has become less useful and less significant in recent years because her successors often don't know whom to ask. Many major critics get left out and/or too many dubious reviewers get included. Phillip Lopate's Library of America volume on American film criticism has the same provinciality, including, for instance, Armond White, but neither Dave Kehr nor James Naremore. It wasn't that way when Penelope was at *Sight and Sound*. She actually knew who the most knowledgeable people were.

One thing I came across recently was that she wrote a letter to Jacques Rivette asking him to write a piece about the state of the New Wave. He eventually wrote back turning her down. But the fact that she would try to do things like that and was very conscientious about it made her stand apart. In other words, it seems to me that she was sophisticated about film, even if she hadn't seen all the films herself. An awful lot of her competitors were not so broad-minded. When she retired, I thought *Sight and Sound* could go in two different directions. It could become more international or it could become more American. I felt that what they did, to my regret, was become more American. I still feel that this limits *Sight and Sound* because, to me, the radical difference between what *Sight and Sound* is now and what it was when I was on the staff is that today it's totally consumer-oriented. It's just basically trying to review what's out on the market as opposed to what's out in the world—the most common form of capitalist censorship that routinely defers to fashion and the status quo.

What does Jeanne Dielman *being ranked number one in the recent* Sight and Sound *poll of the best films of all time reveal about that magazine and the current state of film culture?*

To me it was proof of how *Sight and Sound* has situated itself as an institution privy to other institutions, like universities and colleges, rather than to individuals.

One of the great tragedies of Anglo-American film studies is that most people who are interested in cinema are split into two factions: academics and non-academics, and they don't bother to read each other. People in academia didn't read people like Penelope Houston, and people like Penelope didn't read people like them. It seemed to me that both factions became provincial as a consequence of not seeing film in a wider context.

Of course, it was a different world in the mid-'70s when I was writing for *Sight and Sound* and the *Bulletin*. You could still believe then that the world of film was one group of people and that you were writing for them. You might even say that this assumption became downgraded by alienated labor, which is how *Jeanne Dielman* wound up replacing *Citizen Kane* and *Vertigo* at the top of the list— a clear sign of deferring to academics and academic fashion over everyone and everything else. And maybe placing political correctness over aesthetics, even though Akerman clearly matters as an artist.

When I conducted a poll about English film taste for the November-December 1976 issue of *Film Comment*, I thought I was addressing myself to both the academic world and the mainstream world. But I don't think that most of my colleagues thought that way. They only thought about joining one group or the other, assuming that you couldn't belong to both.

I'm more resentful of the academic group than I am of the mainstream because I wasted so many years not being hired, or else basically being ruled by people who knew only a fraction as much about film as I did. I didn't have any health insurance or any of the other benefits that the so-called professionals had by being an academic because I didn't have the right degrees. Even when I accepted the job at the *Chicago Reader*, I was told by the University of California, Santa Barbara film program, "It's a good thing you're getting this job because we wouldn't have rehired you." I resented the degree to which I was exploited. Truthfully, the two portions of my career for which I have no nostalgia are grad school and my time teaching in Santa Barbara. The seeming absence of community in both places was stifling.

Do you believe that the gap between the academic world and the mainstream, or journalism, has become wider or narrower today?

Maybe a little wider. I think one of the reasons why I appeal to younger people with my writing is because I don't think that they feel bound to belong to one faction or another.

Writing for Others

Do some of your capsule reviews published in Time Out *date back to the 1970s as well?*

Yes, probably all of them. At the time, the person who assigned the reviews was Chris Petit. He was the lead film critic. I was friendly with him but only belatedly became aware of how ambitious he was, both as a writer and as a filmmaker. I was the one who introduced him to Manny Farber because he made a trip to the West Coast and came down to San Diego when I was there. They wound up becoming good friends, even going on holidays together with their wives.

Years later, when I wrote for the *Chicago Reader*, even though I wasn't under contract—it was just a handshake deal—the understanding was that they didn't want me to write for any other publication in Chicago. When I wrote for a while for an arts magazine based in Chicago called *Stop Smiling*, which was edited by J.C. Gabel—the same person who has just published my new book, *In Dreams Begin Responsibilities*—the *Reader*'s editor objected because she didn't want me to write for them. I ignored her objection because I regarded *Stop Smiling* as national rather than local. It didn't focus on local matters.

But in London, there was no objection to writing for other London publications. Once or twice a year, when the *Financial Times* critic Nigel Andrews went away, there were two different times in two successive years when he asked me to replace him and take over his column.

I remember finding it unfortunate that when I was commissioned by *Time Out* to write a cover story about Jerry Lewis, defending him as a filmmaker, the title they gave to the piece, which I and various other people found offensive, was "Auteur or Idiot?"

Were you in any way influenced by the English tradition of film criticism during your time in London?

Raymond Durgnat definitely was an influence, and so was Tom Milne. Those were my two main influences, even though the two of them had contempt for each other. Everything became so factionalized in London.

Tom Milne

In what way did Tom Milne influence you?

First of all, he was a very good translator. He translated all of Godard's criticism and subtitled *Les Demoiselles de Rochefort* in rhyming couplets for the BBC. I think we had very similar tastes about some things, and where we disagreed, he could be totally unreasonable. He and Richard Roud both hated Tati. They thought he wasn't funny and was therefore devoid of interest, so we never really had a coherent discussion about Tati. But for the most part, Tom was a very thoughtful person. He and I went to a lot of screenings together and talked about the things we were writing about for the *Bulletin* and *Sight and Sound*. Tom's enthusiasms always made him seem more French than English, at least temperamentally.

He eventually just gave it up and, like the way I live in Chicago, became very reclusive. He got so little feedback about his work that he gave up being a critic and went back to Scotland, living with his sister until he died—which is sad. He taught me a great deal, and I think it's a scandal that his best writing for *Sight and Sound* and the *Bulletin* has never been collected.

Even though he wasn't on the forefront of theory like the *Screen* people, Tom was very bright. When I was given the assignment of translating André Bazin's book on Welles, he volunteered to check everything and refused to accept any payment for his work. In other words, he went through all my translations, corrected my mistakes, retranslating where necessary. He did all that to make me look good, which was very generous of him.

Did you have a lot in common when it came to Carl Dreyer?*

Yes, even though we saw Dreyer in different ways. It was after I was at the BFI that I wrote my piece on *Gertrud*, but that had been a piece I'd been thinking about and researching for years.

Raymond Durgnat

How was your relationship with Raymond Durgnat in those years?

I also should say that, on my own initiative, I looked up and befriended Ray Durgnat when I was living in London, but it took a while before he really trusted me. He had a paranoid streak, particularly against *Sight and Sound* and Penelope, even though early on he'd actually written for the magazine. But after our paths crossed again in the States—first in New York, then in San Diego—we became good friends. We even became housemates in Del Mar, a San Diego suburb.

Would you say that Durgnat's writing style is less accessible compared to yours? And is one of the reasons you have a wide range of readers around the world the way you write?

---

* Milne wrote and published a book on the Danish director, entitled *The Cinema of Carl Dreyer*.

I suppose that's true. Accessible or not, I have to say that Ray was a very interesting critic, but he tended to be boring as a teacher. That's my sense, from the students and from the classes of his that I visited or attended. I think I'm a good teacher now, but I had to learn how to be good. When I first went to substitute for Manny Farber as a lecturer at classes with high enrollments, I was a flop—a real flop. It wasn't something that came naturally to me, but it's something I feel that I know now, and I feel much more confident about doing.

One of the things that I was so delighted by is that before Ray Durgnat died, when he was in a hospital, I sent him videos of movies to watch while he was there. He died even before he could watch any of them, but I talked with his brother, and he told me Ray was very happy when he died. That really had a big impact on me because that's something you don't normally hear—that people are very happy when they die. It was true of my brother Alvin, whom I was very close to. He actually built his own coffin months before he got sick. I thought: Everybody has to die. Everybody is born, and they don't feel bad about being born. So why do they have to feel bad about dying? If everybody dies, it's a losing proposition if everybody feels bad about it. I thought I learned a lesson from that, and it was a lesson that indirectly both Ray Durgnat and my brother Alvin taught me.

Scénario(s)

I felt the same—a lesson to be learned—when I recently watched Scénario(s) *by Godard. The second half of the film, the MRI version, moved me enormously, and I was somehow comforted by its way of embracing and even poking fun at death. As Jean Yanne says in* Weekend, *"These idiots are all dead." What are your thoughts on this relationship with the filmmaker's death?*

Thanks for telling me this. Godard's *Scénario(s)* has so far mainly struck me as opaque, but your observation makes me want to go back to this final work to see and hear it the way you do. That's what the best criticism always does.

Peter Wollen

What do you think of Peter Wollen?

I met Peter the first time I ever went to London, when I was editing the anthology of film criticism I had been commissioned to do. That was before I became a film critic or had any sustained ambition to become one. Peter was working at the BFI and invited me to meet him at a pub after work. I think he considered me naïve when it came to his turf, film theory and stuff like that.

A film that had a big impact on me when I saw it for the first time at the Edinburgh Film Festival was Lev Kuleshov's *The Great Consoler.* I found out later that the only reason they showed it was that Peter had suggested it, without having seen it himself. But one annoying thing was the way the festival used him as a filter for what they should and shouldn't show. If he hadn't mentioned a filmmaker or film in one of his essays, it couldn't get into the festival. That, at least, was the situation as I perceived it. I found it amazing how even people like Peter seemed very provincial about certain things. It seemed that the reason they were reluctant to show any film by Rivette was that Peter had never written about him. They were that conformist, or, at least, it seemed that the festival's artistic director, Lynda Myles, was very reliant on Peter rather than on her own taste, which I thought was unfortunate.

I campaigned and was eventually successful in getting Rivette's *Duelle* into the festival, but the fact that they showed it at all was controversial. Almost all the writers at *Screen* put it down and insisted that it was of no interest. Many of them reacted at the festival to Ken Jacobs' *Tom, Tom, the Piper's Son* like total philistines. They were saying, "Oh, what is this shit? I'm leaving!" In other words, they had the same kind of reaction to experimental film that dumb Americans or French teenagers would have. It was very discouraging.

Years later, when I was talking to Peter about Orson Welles and mentioned the book by Welles and Peter Bogdanovich that I had edited, *This is Orson Welles* (1992), Peter said he'd never heard of it, despite his special interest in Welles. That struck me as a little bit dismaying, especially because so many people deferred to him as an expert on such matters.

Also years later, I discovered that Laura Mulvey, whom I had known somewhat better when I was living in London, didn't know about the existence of my book *Moving Places* that was published only three years after I returned to the States. I was a little put off that she didn't know that I'd grown up in a Frank Lloyd Wright house. She could tell I was a bit upset, and she said she was going to get the book. I don't know if she did or not. But the point is that these people lived in very narrow circles and had fewer reference points than the people I knew in France — or so it seemed. I had friends who used to refer to Peter and Laura as the Royal Family, a joke that may have been partially inspired by Laura's upper-class accent.

London vs. Paris

How would you compare the London repertory cinema scene of the 1970s to that of Paris?

Really no comparison. I had an English girlfriend at one point in Paris who was getting her PhD in French literature but was also a film buff. We met at a revival of Fritz Lang's silent *Dr. Mabuse*. For her, going to a double bill was always better than going to a single feature. In other words, it was sort of "get more for your money" — more bang for your buck. Much worse than that was a young woman I knew in London who taught film and would show clips in her classes from films like *Gentlemen Prefer Blondes* without ever bothering to see the entire film. For teachers trained by the BFI's Education Department, this was typical rather than exceptional.

The atmosphere in France was more intellectual. It seems to me that the people I knew in London, including the film buffs, were not intellectual in the way that the Parisians that I knew were. And, of course, this was during the period when *Cahiers du Cinéma* was at its most left-wing and academic — in other words, when they became more heavily into film theory. Penelope clearly had less interest in film theory and she obviously was attracted to prose that made such things more comprehensible.

And fewer classic films were shown in London compared to Paris?

Yes. For sure. They were not even comparable. The first time I was ever in Paris, they were showing Dovzhenko's *Aerograd* at several cinemas in brand new prints, as a re-release. Something like that would have been unthinkable in the U.K. or the U.S. In London, you could maybe see a Buster Keaton retrospective at the Academy cinema, but getting new prints of any Dovzhenko film wouldn't even be considered. I felt that moving from Paris to London was, in a lot of ways, definitely a step backwards in terms of film culture, even though I was in a much more privileged position in London than I had been in Paris.

Céline and Julie Go Boating in London

You must have found this very frustrating in London.

Yes. For instance, I was very eager to help find an English distributor for *Céline and Julie Go Boating*. But no one was willing to release the film until finally, one distributor, Contemporary Films, said to me, "Okay, we'll distribute the film on one condition: that you prepare the pressbook for us free of charge." And I agreed to those terms.

And so the only time in my life I ever put together a pressbook singlehandedly (for *Touch of Evil*, I collaborated with Rick Schmidlin, producer of the re-edit) was the one I did for Contemporary. What amazed me was that the week the film was released and I looked up all the reviews, I discovered that many reviewers, including even ones who disliked the film, were plagiarizing whole sections of my pressbook verbatim. I was shocked to discover the extent to which critics were not even interested in supplying their own prose, but were quite happy to copy things from the pressbook.*

When I was working at the *Bulletin*, there were so many films about which very little had been written. Particularly when it came to porn films, sometimes I had only one source for writing a plot description, so that was a kind of soft plagiarizing, rephrasing some sentence written by a publicist.

The way that reviews are commonly done in London's daily press is to cover all the major releases in one weekly column. I've done that myself for the *Financial Times* and more recently for the *Chicago Reader*. This has always struck me as an alienated approach to film reviewing, flip and superficial. You wouldn't find that kind of thing being done as crudely in Paris.

---

* In 2012, I discovered that Jonathan's *Monthly Film Bulletin* review of the 1929 Duke Ellington film, *Black and Tan* (or *Black and Tan Fantasy*, depending on which print of the film one refers to) was shamelessly plagiarized in *Duke Ellington and His World* by A.H. Lawrence, published by Routledge in 2001. A comparison of Jonathan's original text and the plagiarized version—which often doesn't even bother to alter some of the words—can be found on my jazz blog, Take the "A" Train.

When Céline and Julie *was released in London, were you still in touch with Rivette?*

Not directly with Rivette, but with Eduardo de Gregorio, who was working for him as a writer. In fact, while I was at *Sight and Sound*, I proposed writing a big piece about the shooting of Rivette's *Duelle* and *Noroît*, the first two in a projected quartet of experimental features that was never completed. I enlisted both Michael Graham, Eduardo's American boyfriend, and Gilbert Adair, a Cinémathèque chum, to cover other portions of these successive productions, shot back-to-back in Paris and Brittany respectively. This huge piece had four parts: me writing the first and last parts, and Gilbert and Michael writing the two parts in between. So I guess you could say that I became the equivalent of a guest editor in some ways.

BFI Wars

There is a picture of you in front of the BFI building demonstrating. What's the story behind that?

One of the first things I did when I went to work for the BFI, in the late summer of 1974, was that I joined the union. I went to my first meeting in which we were voting on whether to go on strike because Kevin Gough-Yates had just been fired as a director of the BFI without the proper procedures being followed. I basically seconded the motion for us to go on strike, and wound up on the picket line, which is how I got to know many people at the BFI. It was funny because Penelope Houston, although she wasn't a member of the union by any means—she was management—would come and deliver our mail that had arrived that day while we were on the picket line. It was an exciting time for me. I had already met Otto Preminger because I'd watched some of the shooting of *Rosebud* in Paris before I left, and he was editing that film next door to the BFI on Dean Street. I got him to sign our petition supporting our strike, which we eventually won. I mean, we got most of what we wanted. Vanessa Redgrave visited us in front of the BFI and tried to get us to start fights with the police. I remember Colin McArthur[*] actually crossing the picket line quoting Engels.

---

[*] Colin McArthur (b.1934). Head of BFI Distribution division (1968–84) and author of *Scotch Reels: Scotland in Cinema and Television* (1982).

It's interesting, because I thought Colin McArthur was into unions and basically a man of the left.

But he was the head of the Education Department, just as Penelope was head of Editorial. It had something to do with his position, even though he was a communist.

McArthur writes that different bodies of the BFI were at war with each other like Chinese warlords.

Yes, absolutely! And some of the nature of the battles was quite fascinating. For instance, when Peter Wollen worked for the BFI and was involved with editorial as well as the Education Department. He and Penelope both edited separate books for the Cinema One series. The big difference between them was that the author of any study of a director that Penelope Houston edited would be asked to write about the films in chronological order. With Wollen, the author had to organize their discussion of the films outside chronological order, with a separate connecting thread.

Screen and Tribal Wars

You had friends in, and collaborated with, different clashing groups and fronts, including Screen *magazine.*

I was the only person at the BFI who worked for *Sight and Sound* in the editorial department and was friendly with the people at *Screen*. *Screen* and *Sight and Sound* hated each other. They were ideological enemies. For the most part, I was deliberately defying the barriers, attempting to bring about some sort of truce or peace between them, but the fact of the matter was it was a mutual dislike that wasn't accompanied by any desire to know any more about the opponent. It wasn't like I was going to convince Penelope to sit and read *Screen* or *Screen Education*. Stephen Heath and Colin MacCabe of *Screen* were just as resistant to acknowledging or reading *Sight and Sound*, which was considered "the establishment." But what the *Screen* crowd didn't realize was that Penelope was much more open to the wider world outside academia than they ever were. I was automatically branded by them because I was working for her. People like John Coleman in *New Statesman* would only write about the *Screen* people to say how pretentious he thought they were.

Part of the problem is that English film culture is more harmed by conformity than any other film culture that I know of. In the English film world, a lot of people basically decided that Penelope Houston was a bad person and *Sight and Sound* was a bad object, even if they didn't read the magazine.

A book by Pam Cook published by the BFI came out, and everything that was listed in the bibliography of recommended reading had only one qualification: that every entry must not be something that came from *Sight and Sound*, which meant Pauline Kael was privileged over Bernard Herrmann on the subject of *Citizen Kane* because the latter was interviewed in that evil magazine and therefore couldn't be trusted.* In other words, it was both systematic and very stupid, like Jim Crow in the South. It eliminated everything I wrote too, because I was obviously in league with The Enemy. It was so annoying to have to cope with that nonsense.

I was also annoyed with *Screen* because they would talk about being radical, but they weren't. I went to their meetings—they would have one open meeting a month—and I would say, "Look, if you really want to be political, there's all this censorship going on about the films by Ōshima and Pasolini." It was around the time of *Salò* and *In the Realm of the Senses*, and I was suggesting there should be a demonstration in front of the censors' bureau. But they weren't even remotely interested. They were armchair Marxists. So I was on the wrong side of both factions, as it turned out, by trying to be a middleman.

Did I tell you the story about bringing Ben Brewster into the *Monthly Film Bulletin*?

No, you didn't.

Ben was the main editor of *Screen*. He had taught himself some Japanese in order to better understand Ozu's films, and when we were reviewing some of Ozu films in the *Bulletin*, I thought we should ask him to write something for us. The problem was that when it came to doing a synopsis, he insisted on writing a sequence-by-sequence rundown, which meant his synopsis was five times longer than the average one. We had to reject it and do one of our own. In other words, that was an experiment that didn't last long, and we had to do a lot of heavy editing before his review was finally deemed publishable.

One of the more popular things that I did—let's call it a gesture of trying to bring the different factions together—

---

* *The Cinema Book* (1985).

was when I did a survey for *Film Comment* on the favorite films and texts of various people on the London film scene. I got people like Laura Mulvey and Colin MacCabe—in other words, *Screen* people—as well as various people at the BFI involved. That was very revealing because it showed how much uniformity there was within separate factions.

It annoyed me that the people on *Movie*,* too, automatically considered me tainted because I wrote for *Sight and Sound*. I guess what was controversial for some people about me being on the staff was that the BFI had to convince the government that I could do the job and that nobody who was British could, which was a ridiculous thing to argue.

Everything in London was club-oriented. You were always a member of a club, whether it was official, like the people at *Screen* or *Movie*, or unofficial. Everything was structured that way. Part of what made life in London difficult for me was I didn't have a club of my own. I was identified with the BFI, so I was a member of that club, but only by default. I was even a member of their union, so I did feel part of that, and it was fun getting to know other members when we were on strike together. But the point is that I didn't have a kind of social club that represented my aesthetic or intellectual interests. And so, in that sense, I felt more isolated than I'd been in Paris, where I was friendly with people like Raymond Bellour and Bernard Eisenschitz.

This was one reason why my days in London became numbered, because I decided to put myself in between these warring tribes. I tried to bring them together, but it didn't work at all.

English film culture can be very provincial in a lot of ways, and still is, I think. French film culture can be provincial too because there are a lot of things that don't get recognized unless they appear in French. I probably never would have been praised by Godard if it hadn't been for the fact that I wrote for *Trafic*.

The fragmentation you refer to—did it also exist when it came to book publications?

I think one can argue that the BFI Classics books have had at least as good an overall track record as the Seghers series in France—which is devoted to directors—did. But one other consequential meeting I had during that period came

---

* A British film magazine established in 1962 by Ian Cameron. Some of its most important contributors were Mark Shivas, V. F. Perkins, Paul Mayersberg and Robin Wood. In 1966, *Movie* began publishing a series of books by authors including Wood, Raymond Durgnat and Peter Bogdanovich.

when Peter Gidal put together a book called *Structural Film Anthology*, which he submitted to the BFI. At an editorial meeting, I argued on his behalf, even though I didn't like his own films. I thought at least his positions, which were quite extreme, were very interesting. They said, "Okay, if you can make his essay and introduction explicable to us, we'll publish it." That's how Peter and I became friends.

I do remember at the time something that was really annoying to me about Paul Willemen, another person at the BFI who basically had his foot in two camps because he worked for the BFI in the Education Department but was also on the editorial board of *Screen*. He took my advice about including Roland Barthes' piece about *Salò* in his collection devoted to Pasolini, an essay he hadn't known about, but wouldn't dream of including me in his list of acknowledgments. That wasn't a big deal in itself, but then he told me he was willing to vote for the BFI publishing Peter Gidal's book only if he was thanked in that book's acknowledgements. In other words, a double standard based on pettiness. Basically, for him, giving him an acknowledgement in the Gidal book was showing that he was part of the right tribe because he supported the English avant-garde. It's all about his own credentials. So much of what happens in the English film world is, or at least was, in my experience, about paranoia and pettiness. But maybe my remembering and citing all this makes me petty as well.

Cy Endfield

Did you have any encounters with American exiles in London, like Joseph Losey and Cy Endfield?

The only time I met Losey was very briefly at the Venice Film Festival, but I knew Endfield better.

How did you become acquainted with him?

That was later on, when I was living in Chicago. After I wrote an article about him, he saw it and reached out to me. We had a long phone conversation, and eventually I spent a night at his house in the U.K., talking with him all day.

Did he live in London?

No, it was very much in the wilds of England. I can't remember where, but it was far away because his wife liked living in the country. I actually got a ride from my brother Michael and came back to London on the train. He was trying to pitch the idea of me writing or co-writing his autobiography. He was half-blind then, or two-thirds blind, and felt the only way he could do it was with me. My problem was that I didn't think I'd be able to sell it because he was so unknown in the States. He thought that what made his book saleable was that Marilyn Monroe had been his assistant when he had been a magician, but somehow that didn't seem sufficient to make his book something I could sell to the American public.

He told me that he didn't feel especially virtuous as someone who hadn't given names during the McCarthy era. I later discovered from Brian Neve's excellent biography that there was a period after he moved to the U.K. when he offered to give names because he couldn't find enough work, but by that point HUAC wasn't interested, which was pathetic. After his success in British cinema, he went back to the U.S. hoping to be noticed, but that never happened. This was obviously something he was embarrassed about when I met him during his final years in England.

Joseph Losey

Do you care for Losey's British films?

I have mixed feelings because I have mixed feelings about Harold Pinter. I was quite impressed by *The Servant*, but didn't care for *Accident* as much. I also had an unpleasant experience with Losey at the Cannes Film Festival. When they showed *The Go-Between*, I said at the press conference that the way it handled point of view reminded me of *What Maisie Knew* by Henry James. When I asked if they'd been thinking about that novel, Pinter very angrily said, "The script is based on a novel by L.P. Hartley." Losey then said, "I expect the next question is going to be, 'Were you influenced by Proust?'" They were very scornful, but it seemed to me that my question was really about the way their narrative was structured.

My favorite Losey film is *These Are the Damned*, also known as *The Damned*, the sci-fi film, which has never been high on most people's list. I think it's quite an extraordinary film in many ways. Certainly he was an interesting and important director.

There is something else I can mention, which is an embarrassing story. My first time at the San Sebastián Film

Festival, during the Franco regime, I was on a bus going to Pamplona because the guests of the festival were treated to a free trip to the bullfight. I was talking to Derek Malcolm and said that one thing I really didn't like about Losey/Pinter's British films was their kind of nastiness. Malcolm got really annoyed and said, "But they're not English. Pinter is Jewish." I thought that was revealing of a certain kind of anti-Semitism on Derek Malcolm's part. Then, as soon as he said it, he was clearly embarrassed. Anyway, I mention that anecdote partly in order to say that I was not part of Losey's cheering section.

Too Much Rain

Did you cope with the London weather?

Whenever I had to wait for my bus at Chelsea's World's End, standing in a cold rain, it used to drive me crazy noticing how cheerful everyone else was, as though standing in this rain was a delightful experience. I would feel guilty and alienated because I didn't share their delight.

When you were in Europe, was going to museums and galleries part of your regular activities, or were you more consumed by attending screenings and writing about movies?

My visits to museums and galleries were infrequent. Part of that had to do with my social life, the friends I had. Almost everybody who has a social life in Paris belongs to some clique or another. I had my own clique in Paris, which consisted of Eduardo de Gregorio, a woman named Lauren Sedofsky, and Gilbert Adair. I was the only straight person in this group; all the others were either bi or gay. What I did had a lot to do with what they did. I recall going to see Sondheim's *A Little Night Music* with Jean Simmons at a London theater with Eduardo, Michael and Gilbert, all of whom left during the intermission, while I stayed.

Their French, to a certain extent, was better than mine, and one reason why I asked Lauren and Gilbert to interview Rivette with me was because I didn't feel I could handle it on my own. It's been a lifelong disability that I've never been able to become fluent in any other language, even though I've tried. It's a disability that my brothers have shared, including my brother Michael, who was married for decades to a French woman and never learned to speak French. My brother Alvin, who lived in Costa Rica for a few years, never learned Spanish while his wife became fluent. No matter how hard I tried, I never managed to become bilingual. Perhaps my father's habit of reading to my brothers and me so often left us spoiled and a little lazy.

BACK TO THE U.S.A.

What motivated you to pursue a position in the States?

Partly homesickness as an American. And I think what had happened was the second time I went to Edinburgh and wrote coverage for *Sight and Sound*, I was in a more embattled position than I had been before.

In effect, one might say that I'd painted myself into a corner so that I wasn't accepted as either part of the *Screen* or *Sight and Sound* groups. Penelope was getting more upset about me defending *Screen*, or at least defending what I thought was the intellectual cogency of some its positions. Of course, I was attacking them in certain respects also. In addition, I was getting worried that I was losing touch with American speech and that somehow that had something to do with my ambitions as a writer. None of this was fully articulated. I didn't have the slightest idea that I would end up writing something like *Moving Places*. That only came later, once I was back in the States.

When I moved to Paris, it was definitely because of my desire to live in Paris. But I've never been an Anglophile, and despite all the perks of my job at the BFI, I was finding it harder to imagine an agreeable future in London. I struck a geyser when I sent a letter to Manny Farber and he came back with an offer. I left London for good in early 1977.

University of California

How did you learn about the job opening at his university?

I'd sent a few letters to people asking if there might be a teaching position that they could consider me for. Manny was one of them. We'd spoken on the phone and exchanged letters for that book I edited that never came out, so I wrote to him not even knowing if there was a position that might be available. This was around the time when he received a Guggenheim, and he needed to find somebody to replace him while he was supposedly working on a book that he wound up not working on.

It was kind of weird that my arrival in San Diego coincided with the end of his career as a writer, apart from one piece that he wrote on *Jeanne Dielman* with his partner Patricia Patterson. It was almost like I officiated over his retirement from criticism, which bothered me because he was very competitive in the way he thought about things.

He and Patricia were writing about *Jeanne Dielman* while I was writing about Luc Moullet for the same issue of

Film Comment. I wanted to show my piece to him, and later, while I was writing it, I wanted to show parts of *Moving Places* to him. I lent it to Patricia, and he returned it a few days later with "Sorry, we're too busy." There was even a way in which his competitive attitudes indirectly poisoned my relationship to Jean-Pierre Gorin,* who taught in the same department.

Gorin has considered me ever since then as his mortal enemy, and I still can't understand why. The only thing I ever did which you could say was against him, apart from disagreeing with him when he visited one of my classes, was when I was subletting a house in Del Mar with Louis Hock† and Raymond Durgnat. Gorin wanted to move in with us and I thought it would be too crowded, so I said no, and ever since then he's treated me as an enemy. People say, "He's just screwed up. Don't worry about it," but I still don't understand why. When he gave a big party for Godard while I was in San Diego, I was the only person in the film department who wasn't invited. And Tom Luddy,‡ who thought that behavior was outrageous, made a point of picking me up and driving me over to hang out with Godard to sort of make up for that, which was a very nice gesture. This was long before I became friends with Godard or anything like that.

Did you invite any filmmakers to give talks while you were teaching?

In San Diego, I invited Jon Jost and Jim McBride as guest lecturers and tried to get Tex Avery, who wasn't able to come, but I spoke to him on the phone and he was wonderful. In Santa Barbara, I did events with Robert Wise, about *This Could Be the Night*, and Larry Clark, about *Passing Through*, and when I taught a Welles course, I got Richard Wilson and Gary Graver to come as guest lecturers. Best of all, when I was put in charge of running the summer school shortly before my move to Chicago, I brought Samuel Fuller from Paris to serve as our artist in residence.

---

* Jean-Pierre Gorin (b.1943). French filmmaker and lecturer, best known for his collaborations with Jean-Luc Godard during Godard's so-called "radical" period in the late 1960s and early '70s.
† Louis Hock (b.1948). American artist and filmmaker.
‡ Tom Luddy (1943-2023). American film producer and co-founder of the Telluride Film Festival.

Manny Farber

I would like to ask you about Manny Farber as a critic. What were your thoughts on him at that time, and how do you view him and his writings now?

I considered him the greatest American film critic, and I still do. Something I underline in my new book is that he considered film criticism an art form, and therefore being a film critic was being an artist, and that's one of the main things that I've derived from him.

I have to say, though, as a human being, I didn't like him at all. In fact, I really disliked him. Near the end of his life, he tried to convince me to fly out to the West Coast and go to a painting show of his, and the reason why I wouldn't and didn't is that I had made several trips of that kind over the years and always got abuse in return. I flew all the way from Chicago to New York to attend a lecture of his, and I didn't even get invited to join the group of people who went out to have dinner with him. When he got me to travel all the way to Los Angeles to see to a show of his when I was still in San Diego, and I went around with him, telling him my reactions, he basically said, "You don't understand anything," and basically chewed me out for not understanding his paintings. It was sort of like, "Do I want to go all the way out to the West Coast to look at his paintings and get that treatment again?"

He was full of complexes. The fact that he grew up in this middle-class Jewish family with brothers that were close to each other in age means that we were both victims of extreme sibling rivalry as children. One of the semi-hidden themes of my piece about Manny, "They Drive By Night," is that it's really a piece, in part, about Jewish sibling rivalry. This becomes explicit at the very end of the piece, in which I write, "I won't even tell you what Manny had to say to me about *The American Friend* and *Close Encounters of the Third Kind* on the way back to Del Mar; that's our secret." Even though I didn't analyze or realize it at the time I was writing it, that was me playing a sort of sibling rivalry game. "*I'm* the favorite son, not you." It's the same way my brothers and I would fight for my father's attention. This dynamic between Manny and me is what prevented us from ever becoming close as friends because of the way that he regarded me as a competitor, which seemed to me just ridiculous. How could *anyone* be in competition with Manny Farber? Maybe his competitive streak came from his love of sports.

The funny thing is that both of Manny's two brothers became successful psychoanalysts, so what he did was quite different from them.

He was 25 years your senior, so it's just odd if he had that kind of complex.

The whole thing was absurd. What he expected me to do was to take over his classes. But he was such a singular lecturer. He would have a class of a hundred students and do this kind of free-form lecture, like a jazz solo. I had practically no experience in teaching apart from a small class in freshman English when I was in grad school, and I didn't feel like trying to give an imitation Manny Farber lecture. But then when I taught his critical writing workshop, I found, to my dismay, that his students were trying to imitate Manny when they wrote. I thought that's the last thing he should have encouraged. The important thing was for them to find their own voices. When I told him that, he basically said, "Well, yes, of course," but he seemed kind of embarrassed, maybe because he hadn't tried to discourage anyone from trying to copy his style.

His own self-confidence was sometimes shaky. When he invited me to go with him on this trip to LA, he was afraid to give a lecture to art students because he'd discovered that he had on two different pairs of socks that didn't match. "Nobody's going to notice that," I said. "Don't worry!" When he lectured, as he did once at the Museum of Modern Art, he would forbid Patricia from attending. She had to wait for him in the lobby.

The tragedy about him was that he was a total believer in the art world, the same art world that rejected him. A film that offended him and Patricia deeply, and that they truly hated, was *F for Fake*. It's a film that basically says that the art world is based on all these premises that are not valid. Manny considered many of them valid, even if they rejected him.

I've referred to him as a conservative, which I guess he was, but he actually claimed that during the '30s, at one point, he wanted to join the Communist Party, and the Communist Party wouldn't accept him. That's the story he told. I don't have any details. It's also worth mentioning that a lot of his early writing is explicitly antiracist. Obviously he didn't fit into any group, which was part of the personal problems that he had throughout his life.

For how long were you in charge of his classes?

When he offered the job to me, it was for two quarters, and he said there was an outside chance of me getting rehired for a longer stretch. I wish I still knew where his letter was because it was the only one I ever got from him. It was full of typical Farber prose, so it was a great letter to have received.

I thought it was worth the gamble of coming back to the States, partly because I would be his substitute, which was very exciting to me because he was the critic in the United States that I admired the most.

Did it help you in any way when Raymond Durgnat joined you in San Diego? Was it a good distraction from the tension with Farber?

Absolutely.

Moving to New York

What happened after the teaching gig?

It soon became clear that I wasn't going to be rehired. One thing that really annoyed me was that they didn't even bother to tell me, probably because Manny was too embarrassed. They just sort of ended the quarter without having a faculty meeting to decide my fate, and I had to raise a fuss before they would tell me anything. It was very messy and awkward.

A bit later, somebody told me that the National Endowment for the Arts was giving out grants to film scholars, and it would be a good time to apply for one. I did, and wound up getting a $5,000 grant. On the same day that I learned that I was getting the grant, I first thought about writing *Moving Places*, knowing that I could be supported for the next few months. So I was gainfully employed writing *Moving Places*, meanwhile I stayed in Del Mar, the same San Diego suburb where I was subletting a house with Louis Hock and Ray Durgnat.

During the same period, early 1978, I attended a film theory conference in Milwaukee, where I met and later became involved with a woman named Sandy Flitterman,[*] who was getting a PhD at Berkeley. During a trip to New

---

[*] Today, Sandy Flitterman-Lewis (b.1946) is an associate professor at Rutgers University. She is a co-founder of *Camera Obscura: A Journal of Feminism and Film Theory*.

York, I met a former student of Manny's named Carrie Rickey, the critic who just came out with a biography of Agnès Varda. She said, "You know, if you're looking for a place to live in New York, you could share my apartment," which kind of blew my mind. She only knew me from having read some of my criticism. So eventually in 1978 I moved to New York and spent a year sharing an apartment with her.

Sandy still had to finish her degree at Berkeley, so there was a year when I shared a flat with Carrie in Soho before Sandy could move to New York in 1979 and we could find a place to live. We wound up moving to Hoboken, across the river in New Jersey, because we couldn't find any rents we could afford in Manhattan. We moved into a Hoboken flat where, to this day, she still lives, now with her husband Joel Lewis.

It was difficult living in Hoboken because even though there were charming aspects to it, every time I had to call New York City, it was a long-distance call and my phone bills were enormous. But it was very cheap to go into New York if you took the subway or the PATH train. The bus was quicker but much pricier. Sometimes I ran into John Sayles on the bus, because he was another Hobokenite whose career often took him to Manhattan.

People had a low opinion of Hoboken—even though Frank Sinatra came from there—because it was so working-class. In fact, that's why the last chapter of *Moving Places* is ironically titled "Made in Hoboken." It's also the location where most of *On the Waterfront* was shot.

Jackie Raynal

Was it then that you started working with filmmaker and programmer Jackie Raynal?

Actually, that was a year earlier, in 1978, when I was sharing Carrie's flat on Sullivan Street in Soho. I'd already met Jackie and her businessman husband Sid Geffen when she showed her first film, *Deux Fois* (1968), in Edinburgh. Sid owned two major arthouses in New York, the Carnegie Hall Cinema midtown and Bleecker Street Cinema in Greenwich Village, and Jackie programmed both of them.

When I moved to New York, my first job was working on two separate film programs with Jackie. First, with Carrie, we put together a program at Carnegie Hall devoted to sound in cinema called "Sound Thinking," which was also the title of a solo essay I published concurrently in *Film Comment*. We even wrote notes to hand out at each screening, but due to poor organization these notes never got distributed and the program was kind of a bust.

The next thing I did with Jackie was far more successful. This was a revised version of a series that I had already done at the NFT in London called "Rivette in Context," which I'd done to accompany a collection of his criticism, a short book I'd edited when I was still in London called *Rivette: Texts and Interviews*, although it was published only after I moved to San Diego. The idea was to illustrate Rivette's critical sensibility through both his own films and films by others that had influenced his thinking. You might call it a "critical" program heavily influenced by French criticism. I don't think anyone had done a series quite like that before. Jackie was very much involved because the series even included Jean-Daniel Pollet's *Mediterranée*, a film she'd worked on as assistant editor that had never been shown before in the U.S. In fact, as an editor or assistant editor, Jackie had worked with such figures as Eric Rohmer and Jean Renoir, and from the late '70s through the early '80s she ran a kind of salon out of her Central Park South apartment, holding Sunday brunches for such visiting filmmakers as Chantal Akerman and Marguerite Duras, among many others. During that same period, she directed and starred in *New York Stories* (1980) and *Hotel New York* (1984), both comic and surrealist self-portraits, and I appeared in a cameo in the second of these, playing a pretentious film critic whose discourse parodies *Screen*. Veronica Geng, the film critic I alternated with at *Soho News*, appeared in this scene with me, for which we wrote our own dialogue.

The fifteen separate programs of "Rivette in Context" all had thematic titles.* Plus, there was a plan for a "Special Preview Screening" of *Merry-Go-Round*, Rivette's latest feature, which was cancelled and eventually surfaced much later at the Museum of Modern Art, with Rivette in

---

* The fifteen programs were "Masterplots": *Out 1: Spectre*; "Critical Touchstones (Myth and History)": *The Miracle, Le mépris, Not Reconciled, Mediterranée*; "Critical Touchstones (Documentary and Fiction)": *Something Different, The Edge, Le horla*; "The City as Labyrinth": *Orphée, Paris nous appartient*; "Women and Confinement": *Angel Face* and *La réligieuse*; "Theatre": *L'amour fou*; "Clarke and Rouch": *The Lion Hunters, Les maîtres fous, The Connection*; "Movie Doubles": *Party Girl* and *Gentlemen Prefer Blondes*; "Dizzy Doubles" *Céline et Julie Go Boating*; "A Plunge into Horror": *The Seventh Victim, Cat People, I Walked with a Zombie*; "Menace and Mise en scène": *Duelle*; "Fantasy/Conspiracy": *Moonfleet* and *House of Bamboo*; "Treachery and Mise en scène": *Noroît*; "I am a Camera": *Lady in the Lake* and *Dark Passage*.

attendance. He had been at the NFT's *Noroît* premiere, but not at either of the incarnations of "Rivette in Context."

In fact, it was considered a victory that we got coverage from Andrew Sarris in *The Village Voice* and Roger Greenspun at another alternative paper, even though both of them disparaged the series. In other words, we got coverage, but Sarris was very anti-Rivette. When he met Jean-Pierre Léaud, he was shocked that Léaud had a high opinion of Rivette. For Sarris and David Meeker, Rivette was an amateur who didn't know how to make movies.

During that same period, I picked up part-time teaching gigs, replacing people who were on sabbaticals, like Noël Carroll at NYU for two different courses and Carrie at the School of Visual Arts. Whenever I taught, it would almost always be as an adjunct, although I did have a one-year contract once in Santa Barbara, thanks to the generosity of Alexander Sesonke when he briefly ran the program. That was the closest I ever got to regular employment as a teacher—that and my four two-week stints at Béla Tarr's film.factory in Sarajevo between 2013 and 2015.

From 1978 to 1987 I was basically getting hand-me-downs to support myself, which was in a way why getting the job at the *Chicago Reader* was such a big deal for me. Between the time I was at the BFI and the time I was at the *Reader* was basically a decade in the wilderness.

Jonas Mekas

Did you ever meet Jonas Mekas during your time in New York?

Yes, and I even interviewed him at some length in my commissioned book *Film: The Front Line 1983*.

When I was living in Paris, I remember being told that when MoMA screened Pere Portabella's *Cuadecuc, vampir*, after *The Village Voice* published my review from Cannes, Jonas had a very negative reaction to it, although I don't know why or even if this was true, because I don't believe he ever wrote about it. A decade earlier, he publicly attacked *Last Year at Marienbad* in his *Village Voice* column, saying that it didn't do anything that Stan Brakhage and Gregory Markopoulos hadn't already done earlier and better—which was absurd. He might have felt that *Vampir*, as it was called then, because the Catalan language was outlawed in Spain, was taking too much attention away from the "real" avant-garde, or something like that.

I don't know what the basis of Jonas' objections to Portabella could have been, because I only heard about this secondhand. I hung out with him in Mexico City at a film festival towards the end of his life and we talked about a lot of things, but I never brought up Portabella.

Did Mekas have a political side?

He did, but it seemed to be almost entirely *anti*-political. When I interviewed him for *The Front Line* and I referred to Jack Smith as a political filmmaker, he said, "No, no, he's not political at all, he just carried around that reality in his head." Later, it was confirmed to me by Ken Jacobs that Jack Smith had crossed picket lines, so he wasn't political in any committed way. But it seemed to me that *Flaming Creatures* was still a political gesture. Jonas was standing up for films like that even though Jack Smith hated him for defending him the way he did, because he felt it turned him into something he didn't want to be.

I used to feel more critical towards Jonas because I would go to some of his screenings in New York and I would almost always get dirty looks from him. I felt like his attitude was, "Why are you only showing up now? Why haven't you been a regular?" You know, it was sort of like, "Why weren't you at church last Sunday?" It was almost a kind of a tribal reflex, or so it seemed.

Do you think that his dismissal of Portabella could have anything to do with Portabella's strong political stance?

I suppose the fact that Jonas had suffered a lot for being political before he even came to the United States may have goaded him into taking what he thought was a purely aesthetic position. But I thought there was a strong distinction which he hadn't acknowledged between him and Ken Jacobs, who was very openly and directly political. Even when he talked about what he liked about Ken Jacobs' films, he discussed them in a non-political way, which I think was unfair to them, because they're very powerful as political statements.

Jonas was a real operator in a very effective way. I got to know him well enough to realize that this whole thing about playing the dumb peasant was an act. He came on as if he didn't know anything about art when in reality he was much more sophisticated than that. I think it was something he used as a shield because, after all, he did go to jail for screening *Flaming Creatures*. He was already labeled as political in that way, but he didn't want to be political in other ways, maybe because he felt it would cloud the issues and complicate his positions.

Michael Snow

An experimental filmmaker you championed early on in your career was Michael Snow. What attracted you to his work?

His philosophical bent, his humor, and his versatility as a conceptual artist. His death came so soon after those of Godard and Straub that my commissioned obituaries for all three, included in my last book, are a kind of triptych. Unlike Godard and Straub, he wasn't any sort of cinephile, but he was the only one of the three who became a "real" friend, by which I mean a buddy. After I was sent to Toronto by *Film Comment* to interview him about *Presents* (1981), we used to smoke grass together at his home and then go out for Chinese food whenever I was in town for the Toronto Film Festival—or at least we did this until I published *Film: The Front Line 1983*, which criticized two of his biggest champions: Annette Michelson, deservedly so, and, less deservedly, P. Adams Sitney. But even when our friendship ended, he ended it gracefully.

One might say that Michael was as much an intellectual artist as Jean-Luc and Jean-Marie, but unlike them, he situated himself in the history of art, not the history of cinema. The only part of his artistic activity that I couldn't relate to was his free jazz, although I did once attend one of his weekly jam sessions. I much preferred listening to him play bebop on his piano at home, when he sounded more like a professional musician, which he had been at one point.

Which of his films do you like the most?

My favorite Snow film is probably *Corpus Collosum, in part because it may be his only major film that offers a social commentary, and a social history to go along with it. I reviewed *Corpus Collosum for *Film Comment* in 2002 and for the *Chicago Reader* in 2003. But *Wavelength* (1967) and *La région centrale* (1971) are powerful and singular experiences as well.

Moving Places

How did you conceptualize Moving Places?

When I was in London, I was offered a job of translating André Bazin's book on Welles for Harper & Row. It was very funny that I got that assignment because the people who thought I should do it assumed I would be fluent in French, and I wasn't at all. I wound up hiring friends like Gilbert Adair and Jill Forbes to provide me with initial drafts. Gilbert had already translated Cocteau's "profile" that appears in the book, and I had an extensive correspondence with Truffaut while he was shooting *The Story of Adele H.*, mostly about translating and editing his first-rate foreword to the book. I wrote to Truffaut in English and he wrote to me in French. We only met physically one time during this period, in Mayfair, when he was understandably put off by my meagre French and I was put off by his discomfort, which made him come across like a nervous businessman. Sadly, I think we brought out each other's paranoia—paranoia that eventually was played out in an exchange of letters included in his book-length collection of his correspondence.

In any case, the Bazin book had put me in touch with Cynthia Merman, an editor at Harper & Row, who was not a film buff but had been my main contact. She was the person I contacted about *Moving Places* while I was still living in California.

I think the first things that I wrote for the book were "Prelude," written originally as a column for the September 1977 issue of *Film Comment* while I had an English girlfriend who'd spent the summer with me, and the first chapter, which I also published in *Film Comment*, called "The Plucking of Three Birds of Paradise."

What I used to like most about being a fiction writer when I wrote novels was to have characters who would suddenly start doing things that I hadn't anticipated, so that I was just following what the characters were doing rather than consciously inventing their behavior and actions, as if they had a life of their own. What I wanted to find in *Moving Places* was a book that was like that, where the book would lead me places but that I wouldn't lead the book places, if that makes sense. After I wrote the first chapter, I realized that I needed to go back to Florence and do some research.

What the research consisted of—the larger part of it—was going to the library and going through *The Florence Times* on microfilm to look at all the movie ads, plus my father's columns and what was going on in the world at the same time, and basically filling up a notebook with precise information about this film playing on such and such a date with such and such cartoon, and so on. I used all this information as the springboard, almost like chord changes that I would improvise over, when I wrote the book.

I have to say that I was smoking a lot of marijuana when I was in San Diego, and somehow it was while watching *On Moonlight Bay* again on TV while stoned that I kind of got the idea for doing that long second chapter. I wasn't always stoned when I was writing, and I certainly wasn't whenever I was rewriting or polishing, but pot tended to expand my options and help stimulate my imagination, which is the way my most recent book was written. The advantage of writing while stoned is having fewer restraints and less self-censorship—being freer.

In the middle of writing *Moving Places*, I got invited to give a lecture at the Venice Film Festival, and so the lecture I was giving spontaneously became part of the book. In other words, my life and the haphazard aspects of it would dictate the directions the book would move in. *Moving Places* was very much structured intuitively. The advantage of having Cynthia as my editor was that she wasn't a film buff, so the text had to be comprehensible to her. She was a very good editor in a lot of ways. The one time she didn't let me have my way was when I wanted to include two short stories and two essays by other people as parts of *Moving Places*.

The stories I wanted to include were Delmore Schwartz's "In Dreams Begin Responsibilities" and Thomas Pynchon's "The Secret Integration"; the essays were Charles Eckert's "The Carole Lombard in Macy's Window," a piece about the simultaneous marketing of movies and women's dresses, and Elliott Stein's "My Life with Kong," about his own immersion in the *King Kong* cult. Cynthia read them all and said, "No, this is a book by you. You can't include pieces by other people." But it was very important to me conceptually, partly because I wanted to demonstrate that *Moving Places* was not only or even necessarily just a book about me. These pieces all said and did things that I wanted to say and do myself.

At one point, Cynthia showed me the readers' reports she'd gotten on my book, one of which was so perceptive that the guy who wrote it became a friend—a rather extraordinary person named Paul Schmidt, a poet who was also a highly respected translator of Russian and French literature, including Chekhov and Rimbaud. Paul really understood what I was doing better than anyone else.

Did you get the kind of feedback you expected after Moving Places *came out?*

No. I mean, almost nothing happened, because the book wound up "in turnaround," as Hollywood refers to movies that lose their original sponsors. By the time the book came out, Cynthia had been hired by another publisher and there was no one else at Harper & Row who supported the book or even liked it. I was in a situation where not only would Harper & Row not advertise it, they wouldn't even allow me to place ads for it at my own expense. Some copies were sent out to reviewers, and a few friends reviewed it, like Todd McCarthy in *Variety*, Tom Milne in *Sight and Sound*, and, much later, Ray Durgnat in *Wide Angle*. And Ernest Callenbach, a friendly acquaintance whom Sandy Flitterman-Lewis had worked for in Berkeley, reviewed it sympathetically in *Film Quarterly*. But the reviews in the *Los Angeles Times*, *The Village Voice* and even *Framework* in the U.K. were contemptuous and dismissive. The *Framework* reviewer hadn't even bothered to read it all before deciding it was "rubbish." And I only got reviewed in the *Voice* about a year after the book was published when I convinced a *Voice* editor to assign it to a reviewer. She picked the late Stephen Harvey, who hated it, prompting a lighthearted defence from Veronica Geng in *Soho News* a week later. I was so frustrated that I even wound up reviewing it myself—pseudonymously, as "Nancy Rothstein"—in *Film Comment*. I knew that Robin Wood and Ray Durgnat had at separate times reviewed their own books for *Film Comment* under pseudonyms, so I even developed an imaginary biography for Nancy Rothstein before writing my review: "Nancy Rothstein is working on a book about the Hollywood careers of Eisenstein, Brecht, and Renoir."[*]

I was naïve. I thought the book could serve as a bridge or gateway to me becoming a literary writer. I thought of the book as my farewell to film—a detox journal like *Naked Lunch*. But the book that I'd imagined would appear in the front of bookstores became stuck in the back, in the film book sections. Consequently, the only way I could make a living after the book came out was in relation to film. The fact that I'd fantasized becoming a literary writer professionally turned out to be totally unrealistic.

---

[*] Jonathan clearly chose the name of the influential rabbi from his adolescence for the imaginary Nancy.

Midnight Movies

How did you come to work with J. Hoberman on the book Midnight Movies?

Basically, there was an editor at Harper & Row named Craig Nelson who sent letters to both me and Jim, asking each of us if we'd be interested in writing a book about midnight movies. I wouldn't say that I was a good or close friend of Jim, but we respected each other a lot as colleagues, and we discovered that Craig had sent the same letter to both of us, which naturally made us a little suspicious. I decided to go see Craig first, and I asked him, "Why did you write the same letter to both of us?" Instead of answering the question, he asked me, "Why don't you two write the book together?" As soon as I left Craig's office, I called Jim on a pay phone and repeated Craig's second invitation. He thought a little and said, "Okay, why not?" So that's how it came about.

Neither of us was a particular habitué of midnight movies at that point. Living in Hoboken made it even harder for me to attend midnight screenings in Manhattan, and Jim, in Soho, tended to keep early hours.

We worked on different parts of the book separately and would get together every once in a while, almost always in Manhattan, and compare notes as well as edit one another. But mostly we communicated on the phone. When Jim and his wife and daughter decamped to New England for a lakeside holiday, I rented a car and joined them for a couple of days.

One thing I discovered was that Jim had been edited at *The Village Voice* much more than I had been at *Soho News*. I was hardly edited at all there, but Jim was accustomed to his prose being partially rewritten, which he sometimes did to me and which I accepted. What emerged from this was a kind of house style developed between us, apart from the fact that we were each mostly responsible for individual chapters. As I recall, most of the writing about *The Rocky Horror Picture Show* and *Eraserhead* was mine, and Jim wrote most of the material about George Romero and John Waters.

Midnight Movies is the most commercially successful of all my books, not counting *This is Orson Welles*, which I only edited. It's still in print, although it's no longer published by Harper & Row, which became Harper Collins. Da Capo, a reprint house, reissued it. *Midnight Movies* is the only book of mine so far to have gotten high-profile press overage. It was even reviewed on the front page of *The New York Times Book Review*, although we shared that space with another, unrelated book.

Did your book on Jim Jarmusch's Dead Man *also enjoy the same kind of success?*

Yes. That actually had a second edition, and it's also been translated into three languages. Justine Malle, daughter of Louis Malle, translated it into French, and there are Czech and Persian editions. So yes, it's a cult book about a cult film.

Soho News

How did you end up writing for Soho News?

It was in 1979. Somebody told me that they were about to fire their film critic, Amy Taubin, and I was offered the job of replacing her. Tracy Young, the arts editor, said, "We'd like to force her out and then we can hire you." Amy was certainly not a friend. She had attacked my Rivette series at the Bleecker Street Cinema, calling it a pointless exercise because she claimed incorrectly that I was only showing films that Rivette had written about. I wrote a letter in protest. Earlier she had written something in which she referred to *Screen* as a London magazine that was "fortunately" almost impossible to find in New York City, and I wrote a sarcastic letter saying, "It's so great that we have Amy Taubin to set us straight so that now we don't have to worry about reading Eisenstein or Stephen Heath or Peter Wollen." She replied in the letters column that I was only defending the magazine because it was published by my former employer, the British Film Institute, which was of course a ridiculous stretch. This was typical of the New York turf wars and the sort of antagonism I occasionally encountered.

But in spite of all that, I didn't want to be the cause of Amy being fired. I didn't see why she couldn't stay on as a freelancer while I became the paper's main film critic. And that's what happened. That job supported me because I was writing for them every week, either a book review or a film review, or sometimes both.

Two or three years later, when *I* was fired for unstated reasons (Tracy just stopped accepting my phone calls), Tracy made the same offer to Amy, saying let's force out Jonathan by giving all the assignments to you, and she took it. This happened, in fact, by assigning Amy instead of me to review the first film of her former husband, Richard Foreman. Another petty skirmish in the same turf war.

I think the experience I had at *Soho News* was interesting because, for one thing, as a film critic, I alternated on a weekly basis with Veronica Geng, a humor and parody writer and editor at *The New Yorker*—very bright, not a film person really, but she liked the idea of being a film critic.

Turf Wars

So the turf wars of London also existed in New York?

Yes, and that's why I was finding New York so oppressive. For instance, as I was about to leave on a vacation with Sandy, visiting her twin sister in upstate New York, *Film Comment* contacted me about reviewing the opening night film at the New York Film Festival, Robert Altman's *A Wedding*. I couldn't afford to say no because I needed the money, so instead of being on a holiday, I spent my time in the country writing this piece, which became the lead article for their next issue. But then I wasn't invited to the festival's opening night party, even after I requested an invitation, and to this day, I still have no idea why they chose to blackball me. Of course, the festival is run by the Film Society of Lincoln Center, which also published *Film Comment*, so it seemed outrageous to me that I was being treated as *persona non grata* by the same organization that had just employed me. I even wound up crashing the festival's opening night party in protest.

I was so angry that when I reviewed the Hungarian film *Confidence* in the festival for *Soho News*, I used that review as an excuse to reveal what had happened to me—my lack of "confidence" with the festival. Richard Corliss, the editor of *Film Comment*, wrote a letter back saying he didn't know who did the inviting, but he thought I was being very rude and nasty. I think we both wound up looking awful.

That was an extreme example, but it wasn't the only time I felt that people in New York were waiting for you to die so they could get your apartment. It was that kind of atmosphere. I was very outspoken as a critic then, attacking other people, partly as a result of this poisoned atmosphere, though of course that only made things worse.

Did you enjoy being confrontational?

Yes and no. I mean, there was a kind of heroic myth, like I'm fighting the dragons, and a few friends, like Elliott Stein, took my side. But the consequences were unpleasant. I once wrote a piece for a Canadian magazine attacking Andrew Sarris for his anti-intellectual positions. (He once told me he didn't like Godard's *2 or 3 Things I Know About Her* because Marina Vlady's eyes were too small, unlike Anna Karina's.) The piece wasn't published because I decided to withdraw it, but then I heard that somehow he had read my suppressed article. And I guess he got pissed off when, in my Stroheim entry for Richard Roud's *Cinema: A Critical Dictionary*, I corrected his misstatement in *The American Cinema* about *Foolish Wives* having no camera movements. When I applied to be an adjunct teacher at Columbia University, he vetoed me.

Where does this combativeness come from? To me, your attitude seems closer to the French tradition of film criticism than to the Anglo-Saxon tradition, for example.

That certainly might have influenced me. But I think one thing that's significant about the relationship between Parisian criticism and New York criticism is that they're both geographically very small cities. There's a feeling of crowdedness and there being not enough room or space for everybody. I think that already leads to a certain combativeness and competitiveness. It's paradoxical, because on the one hand you can meet a total stranger in New York and become steadfast friends with him or her almost immediately. It happens at both extremes. People can be very generous, but by and large, particularly if you're in an area that's very competitive, you're seen as a threat.

The experimental and political aspects of *Moving Places* may have also played a role in labeling me a firebrand, and not only in New York. The only bookstore in Florence, Alabama rejected my request to have a book signing there after I sent them a copy at their request.

One of the things I didn't understand in New York was that I thought the critics who had the most power and prestige—apart from *The New York Times*, where the power was institutional—wouldn't mind so much if someone with less of a profile critiqued them, as I had done with Andrew Saris and Pauline Kael. Pauline had even launched her own career by attacking New York critics. I figured they would be good sports about being at the receiving end of such debates, but I was obviously mistaken. I was told I could never hope to be friends with Pauline because of what I'd written about her. I guess people put in positions of power might feel, deep down, that maybe they don't deserve it. The fact that Andrew and Pauline didn't become successful until they were middle-aged might have contributed to this — being haunted by the spectre of their previous obscurity. But I'm only guessing.

So you never got friendly with the two major figures of film criticism in New York?

Andrew eventually became somewhat friendly again, and Pauline did make a sort of friendly gesture towards me when I became a member of the National Society of Film Critics. That was after I started at the *Reader*, when Dave Kehr nominated me, because you had to be nominated and then voted in as a member. Pauline went up to me at the end of the first meeting I attended — there's an annual meeting to vote on awards — and she said, "I want you to know that I voted for you because nobody has attacked me so much in all these years." I laughed and said, "That's because nobody else has *read* you so much." She was a bit taken aback by that and said, "Well, of course you've read me." But then the following year at the National Society, she said, "I was only joking when I said that to you last year. There were other good reasons to have voted for you." At that same meeting she deferred to me when I proposed that we give a special prize — the best experimental film or something like that — to Godard's *Nouvelle Vague*. Even though she had earlier been a big supporter of Godard, her attitude then was: let people who were interested in him, like me, cover his films. She was basically saying, "If you say so, then we should give it an award."

Before all that, I felt that I didn't have a chance of being given a Guggenheim grant because Pauline was on the advisory committee. In other words, I felt I was being blocked in every possible way — a kind of paranoia that probably increased the bad vibes.

Maybe because it isn't considered a center of power like New York, Chicago is much more relaxed and friendly atmosphere. You don't feel that you're in competition with other people. Even though I found Chicago to be relatively boring after New York and Paris, it's a much easier socially, because there's none of that rat race atmosphere.

Samuel Fuller

Do directors with a confrontational style, like Samuel Fuller, appeal to you? Is there an aesthetic quality of combativeness that resonates with you?

I was initially confused about Sam. Before I met him and got to know him, Sarris had referred to him as a "primitive," and that's the way I tended to regard him. Eventually I realized he wasn't a primitive at all. What people were saying was primitive about him came from the fact that he was very working class, and proud of it. He had street smarts. But he was actually, in his own way, quite sophisticated.

When I met him to interview him for *Soho News* about *The Big Red One*, one of the first things he asked me was whether I'd seen Godard's *Made in USA*—which, of course, is dedicated to him, to "Nick and Sam, who taught me to respect sound and image"—and what I thought of it. It wasn't like he was totally puzzled by *Made in USA*, which is one of Godard's most difficult films.

What was even weirder was that I hadn't perceived that Sam Fuller was Jewish until I met him. This might sound racist, but there was something about his body language and his manner that suggested a Jew who'd grown up largely in New York. The moment I said hello to him, I thought, "This guy is Jewish." And of course he was partly in denial about it, but that's because he grew up in a period when it was difficult to be Jewish, especially if you were in journalism or in the Army, before he had the protection of Hollywood.

When I talked to him years later in Santa Barbara about being Jewish (in fact, his father had been very religious, although he died when Sam was very young), Sam said, "Yeah, my father was Jewish, but my mother was Irish." That was total bullshit. His mother liked to drink Irish whiskey but she was also Jewish. The funny thing about this is that it's hard to think of another white filmmaker who was more sensitive to racism and more opposed to it than Sam. I think being Jewish put him in a more sympathetic position against racism in general.

I can remember once telling him the story of how my father almost got fired because my brother Michael was on this civil rights march in Mississippi and spoke to a reporter. George Wallace read the interview and asked the president of Florence State College to fire my father, but fortunately the president refused to do this. Sam said, "Wallace... He's in a wheelchair now, isn't he? *Good!*"

You know, Sam became almost like family. I felt very close to him. The last thing I did at Santa Barbara before I left for Chicago was direct the summer school there. I had enough money in my budget to invite an artist in residence, and I picked Sam and flew him over from Paris. I programmed a Fuller retrospective on campus and arranged for him to visit every summer school course at least once, and for each course to show one of his films. We had dinner every night with other faculty members and we'd invariably close the restaurants because he was such an irrepressible raconteur. Then, just before he flew back to Paris, we were invited to do a couple of Q&As at Berkeley's Pacific Film Archive. He asked me then if he could read *Moving Places* and I found him a used copy at one of the campus bookstores. When I saw him next in Paris he gave me his critique of it. He thought I should have picked a movie to write about that was better known to an '80s audience than *On Moonlight Bay*. We remained close for the remainder of his life, and I dedicated my second collection, *Movies as Politics*, to him.

CHICAGO

How long did it take before you received the offer from the Chicago Reader?

That wasn't until 1986. In fact, they offered me the job a year before I was able to take it because I had just signed a contract with UC Santa Barbara for the very first time to teach for a whole year—something almost unheard of, because I was an adjunct. This had been set up by Alexander Sesonske, bless him, when he briefly chaired UCSB's film program. Because of that contract and the *Chicago Reader* being unwilling to guarantee a year-long contract, I felt I had to turn them down. But I said, "If you're still looking for a film critic a year from now, please try me again." Which is exactly what happened.

As I've already said, the probable low point of my life and career was my time in Santa Barbara, 1983 through 1987, after I broke up with Sandy in '83. The reason I was approached for the *Reader* job, the probable high point, was because of Dave Kehr, who named me as his successor.

Have you stayed in the same neighborhood in Chicago since you moved to the city, or have you moved around?

I've only lived in two places. When I first arrived in Chicago, I moved into an apartment on Wrightwood that the editor who later became the main *Chicago Reader* editor, Michael Lenehan, had vacated because his family was getting larger and he was moving elsewhere. I took over his place and stayed there from 1987 to 1998. After my landlady died, I bought a condo on Buena, which is where I've lived ever since. I wanted something spacious for all my books and videos, with a fireplace and close to the lake, and that's what I have.

You were relieved to move to Chicago?

Yes, absolutely, and the funny part of this was that in my entire life, I think I'd only been to Chicago twice before, as a teenager, en route to other places. I'd once gone by train from Alabama to a Jewish camp in Wisconsin, with a change of trains in Chicago, and I spent most of my time there in a huge movie theater called the Chicago near the train station, watching *Elmer Gantry*, a great movie about the Midwest.

To me, what was representative of what I disliked about Santa Barbara, which many people regard as a liberal haven, was hearing that some restaurant owners would lace their garbage cans with poison to keep the homeless people away. I felt like people expected you to build your own concentration camp, so to speak, and then live inside it. That's how alienated I felt. During my first Chicago winter, when the city had one of its worst blizzards ever, I was absurdly grateful because I figured bad weather made people nicer to one another, in contrast to the glib complacency, snobbery and perfect weather every day in lotus land.

Dave Kehr

Had you met Dave Kehr before moving to Chicago?

Yes, we met every year at the Toronto Film Festival. When I lived in Paris, one of my best friends was an American critic and former English teacher named David Overby, who later became one of the main programmers for Toronto. During that period, 1977 and afterwards, he considered me the best American film critic and basically said to me, "You know, we'll invite you back to Toronto every year, even if you don't write about the festival." An amazing perk, which I also had at the film festival in Rotterdam thanks to Huub Bals. So I was a guest of the festival for the remainder of his life and that was how I met Dave for the first time because he went every year, and had even commissioned a few capsule reviews from me over the years.

We hadn't known each other well, but we admired each other. It was possible to get a free subscription to the *Chicago Reader* then. This was before the Internet, when the only way you could keep up with him as a critic was to get the paper every week in the mail, and they were willing to give out free subscriptions to people who were interested.

Kehr is such a wonderful writer. I somewhat regret that he's now moved to MoMA and no longer works as a critic or writes as much as he used to.

I agree, and I regret that too. But Dave takes a position that's virtually the opposite of mine. I think there's almost a renaissance in film criticism among younger people, whereas he's very dystopian about it. He thinks that it's closer to being the end of film criticism, the end of film as an art form, with young kids who don't know anything about cinema. For him, it's all over, which is why he's not a critic anymore. What he really wanted was to be *The New York Times*' film critic, and all he could get was a position that was in a way more valuable, but to *The New York Times* was less valuable—that column he wrote on DVDs and Blu-rays.

The person who was doing the hiring was my first cousin, the late Joe Lelyveld, the *Times*' executive director, who'd had an enormous influence on me during my teens. During one weekend when I was staying in his flat, he introduced me to both Joyce's *Dubliners* and Baldwin's *Notes of a Native Son*, and my first reading of *Light in August* came about because he'd recommended it.

When Joe phoned me for my input I made a big pitch for Dave, but Joe didn't like his writing. I think the reason why is that he wanted somebody like A.O. Scott, who didn't know more about film than he did. That's the standard position of most American newspaper editors about film critics—a bias they wouldn't dream of having about sports or theater or food or music—because film experts are often regarded as intimidating. I said to Joe, "Well, whomever you hire, definitely don't get anyone who's xenophobic, because if you do, they're going to give negative reviews to my favorite foreign films, and those films will consequently never make it to Chicago." He said, "What?" He'd never heard of such a thing. He was totally unaware that a favorable review of a foreign film in *The New York Times* usually meant that it could then be shown elsewhere. He was totally outside that bubble, unlike everyone in the film world. What strikes me as unfortunate about *The New York Times* is its tendency to operate within a bubble. Not all their film critics fall into this pattern—Manohla Dargis is deeply knowledgeable about film, as was Roger Greenspun in earlier years—but most of the others seem to have been valued more for their lack of expertise than for their insight. It's something that Serge Daney wrote about, that the job of a mainstream critic was to keep the readership ignorant and even make them feel proud of their ignorance. This is related to the notion that everybody's a film critic. When the *Times* hired A.O. Scott, he had published maybe one film review his whole life.

My reputation, such as it is today, largely comes from my two decades at the *Reader*, especially after my reviews started to become available on the Internet. It's such a pity that Dave's long reviews there have never been available online. I think his negative view of film criticism today might have been different if he'd had that exposure.

Chicago Reader

Dave Kehr told me there was a great deal of freedom at the Chicago Reader *because they didn't really care what you wrote. They made their money from ads and listings.*

Their attitude was unusual. I've argued this before and I can say it again: I may have been the only film critic in the United States who had unlimited word count. The longest review I recall writing was a review of Alan Resnais' *Mélo*. The paper's editor said, "We'll publish it all, but don't make a habit of writing reviews this long!" What was even more radical was that I could write about any film as long as it was playing in Chicago. If a film ran in Chicago for six months, I could wait until the fifth month before reviewing it. In fact I did something like that with *Pretty Woman*.

By the time I retired, I no longer had unlimited word count and was expected to review a film the week it opened. All the original freedoms I had eventually went away, which is one of the reasons why I decided to retire when I turned 65.

What was the first review you ever wrote for the Chicago Reader?

Not counting the capsules Dave commissioned when he was still there, once I was actually ensconced in Chicago, the first film I reviewed was *Full Metal Jacket*, and that capsule is in my new book. The first long review I wrote was of a Madonna vehicle called *Who's That Girl?*, but then they held back the release of it so it wasn't the first one that was published. I should add that the *Reader* commissioned three separate long film reviews from me as tryouts when they were considering me for the job. They paid me for all three but ran only one, about Woody Allen's *Radio Days*. The other two were on Bertrand Tavernier's *Round Midnight* and Oliver Stone's *Platoon*.

Ghosts of Vietnam

It's interesting that many of your early writings for the Reader *were related to the Vietnam War. There were a few films about the war released within months of each other.*

Yes, but the only film that was really about Vietnam and came out during the war that I really had total sympathy for was *Winter Soldier*, a documentary in which GIs who committed atrocities confessed to them publicly. I saw that film at Cannes, and in my coverage for *The Village Voice* I cited Thomas Quinn Curtiss' review in the *International Herald Tribune*: "The witnesses disqualify themselves to some extent by their appearances... seeming on sight to be members of fanciful Bohemia. But if there is truth in their testimony, all reputable people will be deeply disturbed."

"Reputable people," I added, "are presumably those who wear ties, shave, go to film festivals, and are thus eminently qualified to comment on the crimes of Vietnam, unlike the badly-groomed slobs who committed, witnessed, suffered, and confessed them." Later on, I was even more incensed about *The Deer Hunter*, a racist, xenophobic film rewarded with Oscars, presumably for saying, "Look at what these awful, evil Vietnamese savages did to our poor, innocent American boys." I found that totally obscene after what the U.S. had done to that country. Then there was *Apocalypse Now*, which I was more sympathetic to, but even there, they used Filipinos in the Philippines as stand-ins for Vietnamese peasants in Vietnam, which is like somebody deciding to make a film about America but using Mexicans to represent vile Americans. As a radical writer named Deidre English pointed out at the time, both *The Deer Hunter* and *Apocalypse Now* invented imaginary Vietcong atrocities—the Russian roulette game and cutting off the arms of inoculated children, respectively—to justify real American savagery.

Hate Mail

Did you receive hate mail when you attacked a popular, mainstream film in the Reader?

Usually, yes, especially on *Star Wars*, *The Silence of the Lambs* and *No Country for Old Men*, all of which represent American war atrocities only metaphorically. I argued that the popularity of *The Silence of the Lambs* had something to do with people's fascination with killers who kill without any compunction or sense of guilt, which is precisely what and who we are when we fight most of our recent wars—or what we like to call "wars," such as our military occupation of Iraq.

I repeated that argument when *No Country for Old Men* came out, and got even more hate mail. I also recall getting hate mail when I attacked *Fatal Attraction*. That was one of the first films I reviewed for the *Reader*, and I gave it no stars. I said that the movie offers the same kind of fun that one can have by participating in a lynching. I got some negative feedback on that. Usually I got no feedback of any kind, positive or negative, but I did find out that the film reviews were among the things people read most in the *Reader*.

Movies as Politics

When you joined the Reader, *was the rating system of zero to four stars already in place?*

Yes, so I had to play along with that. But that was almost the only requirement. I should add that the editors at the *Reader*, who modelled themselves on *The New Yorker*, were mostly excellent. The main problems I had with most of them at one time or another related to my politics and possibly to the perspectives I had due to my years of living abroad. They were liberal, but they considered me an irresponsible radical. The only times I've ever been censored, and it happened I think only twice during the twenty years I was there, were about political issues. There had been an article by Elliot Weinberger, who writes about politics for the *London Review of Books*, though he's mainly a translator, poet, and literary critic. He wrote that George W. Bush had wanted to attack Iraq before the Gulf War, and I believe my citing of this created some friction. On another occasion, I wasn't allowed to say that Iran was as multicultural as the United States, and that this was apparent to anyone who visited the country. The editor said that unless you can prove that statement, you can't say it. If I'd known then about the CIA's website, that would have proven it, but I didn't.* Anyway, I thought my editor was being highly selective about what did or didn't need to be proven.

The *Reader* Routine

Did you also review home video releases?

It wasn't considered part of the job. I did a column on the first season of *Twin Peaks* in 1990, and in 2004 I reviewed a video release, *Outfoxed: Rupert Murdoch's War on Journalism*. But these were exceptions.

---

* The CIA entry on Iran can be accessed here: https://www.cia.gov/the-world-factbook/countries/iran/. It notes the large number of ethnic tribes and languages that can be found in the country.

Did your job require you to go to the office regularly, or could you work from home?

I usually needed to be there, but I liked going to the office anyway. I've always had fond memories of the offices at the Rosenbaum theaters in Florence, and of the office I'd gone to every weekday at the BFI. In Chicago, where the *Reader* offices were also centrally located, I felt it was my community and I really liked that, at least until I was kicked upstairs because I wasn't an editor.

The least enjoyable part of my job was doing the theater listings, which was as mechanical as chasing down film credits at the BFI. It meant calling up the various venues, getting things faxed to me about what films were playing and where, what the actual daily schedules were, and so on, because the *Reader* ran all this information and I was responsible for it. Later I was able to get some help from other people, and once the computers came in it was easier. Originally I was submitting everything in hard copy, but after a year or two, I got a computer and the *Reader* went online.

What year was that?

It probably would have been around 1990.

And did you get your first computer through the Reader *or did you already have a computer?*

I had a computer at the *Reader*. I didn't have one at home until later.

How many cinemas did you have to contact to complete your listings?

Oh God… it felt like dozens, but many of them came in clusters, because several theaters belonged to the same companies. Lots, in any case. Chicago is the third largest city in the United States, and we also covered many suburban theaters, so there was a lot of information to pull together. Originally it was just me covering everything, but obviously one person couldn't do it all, and during the year between Dave leaving and my arrival, there was an editor named Pat Graham who did all these capsule reviews. He never wrote any long reviews, but he was a film buff. Fairly early on, for certain things during a film festival, I assigned reviews to other people. There would also be occasional guest reviews, like at one point Thom Andersen asked to write about *The Crying Game*, and I was able to expedite that.

Did you conduct any interviews for the Reader?

I occasionally talked to people and then would sometimes jot things down and if it was relevant, put it in my review. But in terms of actually running a piece that was an interview, I don't think that ever happened. It happened a few times at *Soho News*, with Godard and Sam Fuller and Ivan Passer, and I interviewed Mark Rappaport, Jim Jarmusch and John Gianvito for *Cineaste*.

Siskel & Ebert

Two of the most popular contemporary critics, at least in America, were Gene Siskel and Roger Ebert, who were both based in Chicago. I presume you had encounters with them.

We usually attended the same press shows. Some Americans think that Roger and Gene were major figures in global film criticism because with their show *At the Movies*, they became TV stars. Even Kevin Lee[*] credits their show for introducing him to film criticism. That must have been the assumption behind renaming the Art Institute's Film Center the Gene Siskel Film Center right after Gene died — a grotesque decision, because Gene wouldn't set foot inside the place if he were still alive. It's funny, but whenever I point out to someone that one member of that team was a genuine cinephile and the other one wasn't one at all, I'm usually then asked which of the two was the cinephile. The format of *At the Movies* made it impossible to ferret out any such distinction.

The show's line producer, the late Andrea Gronvall, became a good friend after she left the show, and my impression from her was that Gene only went to Cannes once and then didn't go back after he discovered he wasn't a star there. Even so, sometimes I sided with him over Roger when I watched the show because he seemed to have more common sense. I liked Roger's writing more, but preferred reading him on subjects other than movies.

Gene once banned me from attending his and Roger's special press screenings after I dissed him in print. The occasion was my reviewing a Jean Rouch program at the

---

[*] Kevin B. Lee (b.1975). American filmmaker, media artist and critic.

Film Center that Rouch himself would be introducing. Trying to explain the limitations of Chicago film culture that made someone like Rouch seem hopelessly esoteric, I wrote the following paragraph:

"A look at the Friday section of the *Chicago Tribune* of October 26 [1992]... reveals, along with ads, the following items, which seem to appear in descending order of importance. (1) A pejorative review of a very bad movie by a famous amateur reviewer, Gene Siskel, whose 'expertise' is largely predicated on his lack of knowledge about and lack of interest in film history. (2) Five more reviews of disposable movies by teenage reviewers whose own 'expertise' is clearly gauged by the degree to which they qualify as budding Siskels. (3) Two more pejorative reviews of very bad movies (including the same one knocked by Siskel) by a professional reviewer, Dave Kehr, whose professionalism is largely predicated on his knowledge about and interest in film history. (4) Two more reviews by Kehr of much more important movies, including Charles Burnett's *To Sleep With Anger*, which Kehr plausibly deems a 'great film,' a movie 'that can stand confidently with Renoir's [*Boudu Saved from Drowning*],' and which Siskel hasn't even bothered to cover in a capsule review."

Ouch!

I guess that was pretty harsh, especially because it was true. Gene didn't speak to me for a long time afterwards, until I attended a local tribute to him and Roger, where Gene prided himself to me on having once given four stars to a Jon Jost film. Anyway, I was always friendlier with Roger, who even gave a blurb to one of my books and was very generous to me in other ways. He had won a Japanese Foundation fellowship and suggested I apply for one myself. I did, and it made possible my second visit to Japan in as many years, only a year after Shiguehiko Hasumi invited me to join his panel about Ozu.

Speaking of teenage reviewers, having them around was a fashionable practice at the time in some mainstream American newspapers, and speaking of *Boudu Saved From Drowning*, I can't resist recounting an anecdote about one of the first New York City press screenings I ever attended, in 1967. Seated in front of me at *Boudu* was an elderly gentleman who was audibly fidgeting and sometimes even scoffing at the film with grunts of impatience and displeasure. Finally, during the penultimate sequence, after the *clochard* Boudu gets married and sails away with his bride in a rowboat, this annoying crank got up and left the screening. A day or so later, when I read Bosley Crowther's unfavorable review in *The New York Times*, I discovered that he had been the crank. He even got the ending wrong because he left before Boudu's boat overturned and the *clochard* went back to being a *clochard*. Crowther assumed the film ended around the same time that he'd left the screening room, declaring that this "terminal" sequence was one of the only things he liked in the film because it reminded him of Renoir's father's painting. Which only proves how accurate the film's aim is in terms of its class provocation. Crowther must have felt like he was the butt of every gag.

Internationalism

You began publishing your top ten lists in the Reader *as early as your first year there. From the start, the list included international films from around the world. How important was it for you to convey that sense of internationalism to your readers?*

It's always been a basic part of me. It's kind of ironic that I've taken this position because I'm so poor in foreign languages, but I think the fact that I spent nearly eight years abroad played a role in this. It also played a role when I was living in Alabama. People from other countries would visit, or I'd get to know them, and that shaped me early on. For example, there was a guy who moved to Florence with his brother from Bogotá, Colombia. He became not only a good friend but almost a member of my household. He would stay over, and I was very close to him growing up.

I've always thought there's an attraction in the way people from other countries see things differently than Americans do. Getting to know them or becoming familiar with their films expanded my options and horizons because it gave me more viewpoints to consider.

After 9/11, when Americans asked, "Why do they hate us so much?" two things stood out. First, they didn't want to know the answer; it was a rhetorical question. Second, even asking that, considering all America has done to people elsewhere in the world, was as ignorant as anything Trump has said. There's a kind of willful ignorance among Americans that I've always wanted to combat.

Many of the filmmakers I admire most—Welles, Chaplin, even Hitchcock—are internationalists at heart. One of the problems with categorizing films by nationality is that many of the greatest filmmakers can't be tied to a single country. Hitchcock and Chaplin, while British, can't only be seen as British. The same goes for Welles, who shouldn't only be seen as American. Even the Danish Dreyer had a Swedish mother.

Talk about nationalities often doesn't reflect the people of a country, only its leaders, and those leaders often don't represent the population. I'd hate to think that American culture is defined by Donald Trump, or even Barack Obama. Nationality, in today's world, seems to exist for the convenience of billionaires, not ordinary people. It controls markets, not humanity.

We have more in common with people worldwide than we have differences, yet our culture emphasizes the differences. The similarities aren't considered vital, and that's a bad situation.

Ishtar, a Political Film

Back to your top ten that first year. You included Ishtar. *Its reputation has grown since, but what did it mean to you when it came out?*

I was on the West Coast, and I remember talking to Beverly Walker, a publicist based in Los Angeles. She told me she was at a screening and got dirty looks for laughing at some of the gags. There was that much hatred against the film. But I'd already been a huge Elaine May fan, ever since my family had an LP of her routines with Mike Nichols in their Broadway show.

When a film that's truly political turns up in the U.S., it's almost never perceived as political. Nobody thought *Ishtar* was a political film at the time—it wasn't even considered as a possibility. I call it wilful blindness.

It's significant that Peter Biskind, an editor and writer who claims to be a Marxist, wrote more about *Ishtar* than anybody else. Yet his biography of Warren Beatty, which includes all that writing, doesn't mention the political aspects of *Ishtar* even once. For him, the film was just trying to imitate the Bob Hope and Bing Crosby *Road* movies, which were implicitly imperialistic. His take was that if Elaine May had done a better job, it would have been more like those movies. But he never takes the final logical step of arguing that *Ishtar* should have been more imperialistic, which would have given the whole game away.

This depoliticizing often happens, for example with Bill Duke's *Deep Cover*, which was very political, and Luis Buñuel's *The Young One*, which was treated negatively or ignored. Again, the politics weren't acknowledged. It's like there's this notion that politics are serious, movies aren't, so movies can't or shouldn't be political. That's the apparent reasoning.

It's ironic because the films perceived as political are ones like The Killing Fields *or* Mississippi Burning.

Exactly. *Mississippi Burning* is a perfect example. It's still shocking to me that a film so deeply ignorant and inaccurate about both the South and the FBI could end up in Roger Ebert's all-time top ten, especially considering that he was married to a black woman.

Take *Dead Man*, for another example. When people dismissed or ignored it, there was almost no recognition of its political dimensions. Criticism becomes a reflection of attitudes, not just about film but about larger aspects of life. So politics are denied, as with Crowther's review of *Boudu*, because they can't be confronted.

"Bad Years"

In one of your annual Reader *lists, you referred to 1989 as "the best of a bad year." How many "bad years" did you experience during your* Reader *years?*

Oh God, I have no idea. The whole concept of a good year or a bad year is bogus to begin with. Being a regular film reviewer means forgetting what you've already said and written, as well as what you've already seen. It's almost about your lack of memory; it's what allows you to keep going. So, in truth, I have no idea. Once I've filed something, I don't think about it so much afterwards.

But were there periods bad enough to make you frustrated with being a film critic?

I was sometimes frustrated by the overall atmosphere, but I now think that when anybody, including me, talks about a year being good or bad for movies, it's criminally naïve. There are so many major films I didn't see at the time and only discovered later. This year, for example, when I had to submit my top ten list to *Sight and Sound*, it was before

I'd seen some films that really mattered to me. Those films might make it onto my list for Roger Koza's website,* which comes out at the very end of the year. When people say it's a good or bad year for film, they're essentially lying, because nobody sees everything, and why make the studios or distributors the ultimate arbiters of what's good or bad? Even in so-called "great years," like the late '30s or early '40s, there were countless films that people only discovered much later. Journalism simplifies things, but this is a kind of simplification that's criminally uninformed.

When someone in the U.S. says it's a bad year for foreign films, all they're really saying is that it's a bad year for U.S. distribution of foreign films, not that the films themselves are lacking.

The Top Thousand

What was the significance of your thousand favorite films, which you offered as an alternative to the AFI list?

Initially, it was just a list of a hundred films. Here's what happened: I wrote a column attacking the AFI's list of the "100 Best American Films" because I found it outrageous, for several reasons. The British Film Institute and the national cinematheques of most countries include films from all over the world. In contrast, the AFI is only devoted to American film, and not just that, but studio films specifically.

The people who suffered the most from their exclusions were filmmakers like John Cassavetes. There wasn't a single Cassavetes film on that list. Essentially, it was a list of the "100 Best Hollywood Films," and it systematically excluded independent films. Another example: when they created their list of the "Best American Comedies," *Monsieur Verdoux* wasn't on it. That also struck me as outrageous.

That column ended up being one of the most popular things I've ever written for the *Reader*. The response was overwhelmingly positive, and as a spin-off I thought it would make sense to create a list of my thousand favorite films in my book *Essential Cinema*.

Even though many people, including ones I admire, dismiss the idea of ten-best lists, I've always seen value in them. Elena Gorfinkel, for instance, wrote a critique of ten-best lists, if I recall correctly.† But for me, when I first

---

* See Roger Koza's annual polls here: https://www.conlosojosabiertos.com/cat/la-internacional-cinefila/
† "Against Lists," November 29, 2019. https://www.anothergaze.com/elena-gorfinkel-manifesto-against-lists/

became interested in cinema as an art—around the time I was a college freshman in New York, in 1961—ten-best lists were crucial to my self-education.

The first issue of *Sight and Sound* I bought featured their worldwide ten-best lists, and that became my guide to learning about film. I sought out the films those critics had chosen. For me, those lists had a significant pedagogical function that isn't always adequately recognized. One of my closest friends, James Naremore, has also defended the importance of these lists. In his collected film criticism he included pieces he wrote for *Film Quarterly*, annual columns devoted to his ten-best lists for certain years.

In a way, ten-best lists aren't frivolous at all, they're serious position papers. When you make such a list, you're essentially saying, "This is where I stand in relation to these parts of film culture."

Shirazi Filmmakers

I want to move on to your 2024 list, which includes The Seed of the Sacred Fig *by Rasoulof. What did you think of that film?*

Of all the films on my list this year, that might be the one I was most hesitant about. I'm still not sure how it's stayed with me. It deals with serious issues and held my interest in a commercial way throughout, but I remember telling Mehrnaz that when it becomes just a thriller toward the end, it takes too much time being just that. I thought less of it at that point. That said, Rasoulof was dealing masterfully with a lot of elements, and it was innovative. I don't know of any other super-long Iranian films. I'm sure they exist, but I haven't seen them.

This is definitely a rare exception. I can't think of any Iranian films that are as long as The Seed of the Sacred Fig.* *Brick and Mirror* by Ebrahim Golestan is one of the longest, at two hours and ten minutes. Interestingly, I saw affinities between Rasoulof's film and Golestan's work, especially themes like ruin, darkness and night. And both men are from Shiraz. One is a commercial film and the other is cutting-edge arthouse, but there are connections.*

That's interesting. I do feel that Rasoulof, even though he's a commercial filmmaker, carries some characteristics of an

---

* 2h 47m.

arthouse filmmaker. That's important. It reminds me of how form and poetry have a relationship, something that's central to Iranian cinema.

Ebrahim Golestan, an Iranian writer and filmmaker whose work you have championed over the years, viewed cinema—as he mentioned to both of us in Bologna—as merely an extension of his writing. Where does he stand for you, as someone who has explicitly bridged these two worlds?

Alas, none of Golestan's writing has been translated into English, as far as I know, so my view of his writing is necessarily limited to the powerful and eloquent voiceover in *The Crown Jewels of Iran* and the dialogue in *Brick and Mirror*. And yet what moves me most in *Brick and Mirror* is the slow, relentless camera movement away from the stricken heroine in a hospital corridor after she interacts with some of the abandoned children nearby. That isn't a moment Golestan can reproduce in any literary way. I guess one could call this "literature by another means," in which the moving camera opens up her grief to take in a wider world, but I can't imagine any movement in Golestan's prose doing anything emotionally comparable. What do you think?

I agree with you about Brick and Mirror, *and I would go even further and say that the most moving moments in his films are pure cinematic expressions, where literature is abandoned entirely. The match cut between the farmer and the priceless diamond in the jewels collection in* The Crown Jewels of Iran *is another example.*

I believe Golestan regretted not making more films—or perhaps not being able to—while continuing to write. He seemed to console himself by claiming that those films were just another form of writing. But they weren't—or at least not entirely.

Feedback

I'm trying to understand the impact that your writing might have had on filmmakers during your Reader *years. Did you ever receive phone calls or letters from directors whose films you had reviewed?*

Jarmusch was once kind enough to say that he liked my reviews of his films, even when they were critical. And Béla Tarr, who usually disagrees with everything said by critics, including me, told me he liked what I wrote in "A

Bluffer's Guide to Béla Tarr," which was written before we met for the first time. I also received a wonderful email from Guy Maddin after I reviewed *The Saddest Music in the World*. He basically went point by point through what he liked, including the fact that I recognized a reference to Laura Riding Jackson, who's not a very well-known writer, and that my review responded to some of the less serious reviews of the film, like Anthony Lane's in *The New Yorker*.

My friendships with some indie filmmakers such as Mark Rappaport and, although I haven't been in touch with her for several years, Leslie Thornton, are partially related to what I wrote about them, although my friendship with Pedro Costa, initiated by him, began before I'd seen any of his work. I temporarily lost Eduardo de Gregorio, Rivette's screenwriter, as a friend after failing to write about *Sérail* (1976), his first feature.

Godard reacted favorably to my review of his *King Lear*, but I only learned about this because he asked Tom Luddy, his producer, to tell me. Before that, Serge Daney told me that Godard loved something I wrote about Welles for the French quarterly *Trafic*, which I suspect was the way he read me most often, in translation.

So I had those two indications of him liking me even before he invited me to join a panel discussion about *Histoire(s) du Cinéma* in Locarno. I was in New York at the time, in the middle of marathon viewing sessions for the New York Film Festival Selection Committee, but our director, Richard Peña, generously allowed me to visit the Locarno Film Festival for a weekend in order to join that panel. When Godard then invited me and other panelists to come to Rolle to see the two latest chapters of *Histoire(s)*, I painfully had to decline because I couldn't escape my New York duties for any longer than a weekend. But a year later, when Godard flew to Toronto with *For Ever Mozart*, he invited me into his hotel room to watch those two chapters plus a third that was more recently completed. This led to me interviewing him about *Histoire(s)* in *Trafic*, a piece that he later used along with a Hollis Frampton essay in a press handout at Cannes.

Another director who liked what you wrote about him and even said so in a DVD extra was Pere Portabella.

Yes, that couldn't have been more gratifying. I'd given a rave review in *The Village Voice* to *Cuadecuc, vampir* when it played at Cannes in 1971—without his presence, because the Franco government had confiscated his passport as a punishment for having produced *Viridiana*. On Second Run features' release of that film many decades later, at the end of an interview, he credits my review for opening the door to his international reputation.

To conclude this history of favorable feedback, I was deeply moved when the late writer and filmmaker Edgardo Cozarinsky phoned me in Chicago from Buenos Aires after reading "They Drive By Night," my essay about Manny Farber, a translation of which was published in *Trafic*, to tell me how much he liked it.

The National Society of Film Critics

Tell me about joining the National Society of Film Critics.

The National Society of Film Critics belongs to—or, rather, is part of—FIPRESCI, which is the International Organization of Film Critics. But the difference between FIPRESCI and NSFC is that you actually had to be nominated and then voted on and elected to be a member of the latter, unlike the former, so it's almost like a VIP club, making it an honor to belong to it.

One year the top prize for the best film of the year went to Steve Soderbergh's *Out of Sight* with Jennifer Lopez. A curious selection, but it was made because there was a split vote between Terrence Malick's *The Thin Red Line* and Steven Spielberg's *Saving Private Ryan*. *Out of Sight* became the dark horse because when people voted, they gave a first, second and third choice, and *Out of Sight* was practically everyone's second or third choice. That's how it won the prize. This demonstrated how silly the whole process could be, because virtually no one who voted believed it was the best film of the year.

Greed

I'm particularly fond of your 1993 book on Greed. *How did that book come about?*

When I was still living in Paris, Raymond Bellour was doing a collection on American cinema and asked me to write for it. I wrote something about *Greed* that I later decided to expand into a short book for the BFI Classics series.

The two books of mine that have sold the least well have been the book on *Greed* and *Moving Places*. And the French edition of *Moving Places* was clearly the biggest flop of all in terms of sales. P.O.L. published it thanks to Raymond Bellour's support, but they didn't advertise it, even though they could have because Godard had praised it in an interview in *Cahiers du Cinéma*. He described it as "a page of America," and, in fact, I think it flopped in France because so many of its details were legible only in terms of American life and culture in the 1950s, making it obscure to a French audience. Even Antoine de Baecque admitted to me that he couldn't understand the book when he interviewed me about it in *Libération*.

One curious thing about the *Greed* book is that a Portuguese translation came out in Brazil and the BFI strenuously denied its existence, even after I acquired a copy and asked them about it. An unsolved mystery.

Maybe it was unauthorized.

Possibly, but my evidence suggested otherwise, even though I've been told that it's poorly translated.

Dead Man and Jim Jarmusch

Why did you pick Dead Man *to write about for the BFI Modern Classic series?*

It was Rob White who did the picking, based on my lengthy defence of the film in the *Reader*. He's a great editor. Later, he commissioned pieces from me when he became the editor of *Film Quarterly*.

One thing that made Jarmusch's film a cause for me is that when it came out, it was either totally ignored by mainstream outlets like *The New Yorker* or was treated unsympathetically and without any acknowledgment of its politics, the same way the American media treated *Ishtar*.

Some of this stemmed from Harvey Weinstein wanting final cut and basically refusing to promote it after Jim refused. We shouldn't forget that at the time, Weinstein was treated in the press like a national hero who could do no wrong. Janet Maslin at *The New York Times* once even told me that Jim should have let Weinstein re-edit *Dead Man*, and her Cannes coverage one year placed more faith in his opinions than those of the festival jury headed by David Cronenberg.

For me, Weinstein's suppression of *Dead Man*, supported by the mainstream, made it a film that was important to defend. It also seemed to me that this was the only Western that actually addressed Native Americans as audience members. Another incentive for writing the book was my friendship with Jim, which started before he became well known. This came about because I was such a big fan of Sara Driver, his partner, whom I'd devoted a chapter to in *Film: The Front Line 1983*. I even thought at the time that she was likelier to become famous than Jim was, based on his *Permanent Vacation* and her *You Are Not I*. This just shows you how far outside the loop I can be.

Even though I am a huge fan of *Stranger Than Paradise*, after *Mystery Train* and *Night on Earth* I felt that Jim was starting to coast a bit as a sort of lightweight entertainer. That's why *Dead Man* represented a turning point. With that film, he became much more ostensibly political. This was equally true of *Ghost Dog*, his next picture. For me these two remain Jarmusch's best films, although I suppose some would opt for *Paterson*. For me, the best of his later films is *Coffee and Cigarettes*, which most people consider light and minor, because it's so well structured and because it deals so honestly with Jim's ambivalence about being a celebrity.

I feel that in a way maybe he has returned to the tradition of his earlier films that are, as you said, small and entertaining.

I think *The Dead Don't Die* is the weakest and skimpiest of all of his features. I find it harder to judge *Only Lovers Left Alive* because it's so autobiographical about him and Sara, even down to the look of their apartment when they still lived on the Bowery. But, like *Coffee and Cigarettes*, it reminds me of one of the greatest critical statements anybody has ever made, something Harold Bloom wrote about *Don Quixote*. He said—and I'm paraphrasing—that Don Quixote is a totally pathetic character, and so is Sancho Panza, but together they know more than we do. I think that's an amazing insight into the greatness of the Cervantes novel, and what might even be called its conceptual minimalism, in spite of its unwieldy length. Of course, minimalism has always been one of Jim's essential calling cards.

Placing Movies

You joined Chicago Reader *in 1987. And if I'm not mistaken, your first anthology of your writing,* Placing Movies, *appeared in 1995.*

That's right. There had been times before when I'd wanted to do anthologies, but I couldn't get publishers interested. It was also important to me to relate *Placing Movies* to *Moving Places*, a book that, as I've said, was almost designed to fail. I remain grateful to James Naremore for persuading University of California Press to reprint *Moving Places* at the same time that they brought out *Placing Movies*, because as their titles suggest, I conceived of *Placing Movies* as a companion volume.

The only original piece written for *Placing Movies*, apart from the introductions and intermediate sections, was "They Drive by Night: The Criticism of Manny Farber." I showed Farber a copy of it before the book went to press for any corrections he might have, and he did have a couple. But then after the book came out, Manny refused to speak to me for a few years, and I couldn't understand why. He just wasn't returning my phone calls. Louis Hock, a filmmaker friend with whom Ray Durgnat and I had shared a house, reported that for Manny it was one thing reading the essay in manuscript and another thing seeing it in print. That's how irrational Manny could be. Or maybe I was being naïve in realizing that I had revealed things about him that he didn't want revealed. I pointed out his vulnerability, which for me was a plus, but for him it might have been a minus. He finally apologized years later and admitted that he'd been unfair.

Mehrnaz Saeed-Vafa

I want to talk about someone who has been a key figure in your life, and mine too, the Iranian-American teacher, critic and filmmaker Mehrnaz Saeed-Vafa. When did you meet her for the first time?

There was a group called the Chicago Film Seminar that met once a month, and was attended mainly by academics. I read part of my book on *Greed* at one of the sessions, and Mehrnaz came up to me afterwards and said that she really liked my writing. That's how we met.

What do you think of Mehrnaz as a filmmaker and writer?

As a filmmaker she obviously has a poetic sensibility. This was already apparent to me as soon as I saw one of her experimental shorts—*Ruins Within* (1992)—about a belly dancer. The film's title already indicates her poetic streak.

I think one thing that's distinctive about her as a film critic is that at least verbally, she's very assertive and very critical, in addition to having exquisite taste. It's part of her personality. I remember when we were both attending the Fajr Film Festival in Tehran, Kiarostami showed us a rough cut of *ABC Africa* on a Steenbeck along with a few other people. The first thing she said to him before anything else was, "You can't call it *ABC Africa* because it's not about Africa. It's all set in Uganda." She immediately went into attack mode before anyone could say anything nice about it. I think that's a characteristic of hers, which may be off-putting to the filmmakers she critiques but it shows a real critical intelligence. It's worth pointing out that she wrote and published the first defense of Robert Bresson in Iran, not long after she discovered his work while attending film school in London in the mid-70s.

I was impressed, albeit also a little bemused, by *Ruins Within*. But the early short of hers that impresses me the most is *The Silent Majority* (1987), a lovely film about exile that's both poetic and political.

One of the things that drew us together is a dual interest in film and literature. That's an Iranian characteristic, but it's also common in France and Russia and Hungary, among other places. Maybe it's significant that when I met her, I was reading part of my *Greed* book. We were talking about our shared interest yesterday. She's thinking about her upcoming retirement from teaching, even though it's not going to happen right away. Thinking about ways of occupying her time, and talking about wanting to belong to a film club and maybe either join or set up a reading group. We both talked about how great that could be. Of course, it would also be great because it would give us more opportunities to hang out together. The fact that she lives in Evanston, at least an hour away from my condo if I take two subway trains, means that we don't get together very often, because she doesn't like to drive and then look for a parking space, but we talk a lot on the phone. I recently convinced her to watch Manoel de Oliveira's four-hour *Doomed Love*, suspecting that she would love it as much as I do, and I was right. With very few exceptions, our tastes in films are almost identical.

Hungary saw film as an art form before France did. But the high status of poetry in both Iran and Russia is also quite striking. It's not something that a lot of people have as part of their orientation towards film, but Mehrnaz definitely does.

Abbas Kiarostami

The two of you co-authored a book on Abbas Kiarostami.

Yes. She proposed the collaboration. She said, I think in an interview, that one of the reasons why was that we'd had a lot of discussions about Iranian films and she thought that would make it interesting. She said she also wanted to do it because I already had an audience and if she wrote a book on her own, people would find it easier to dismiss by saying, "Oh, she just likes Kiarostami so much because she's Iranian." She thought my input would give more credibility to the project. Jim Naremore as an editor was then starting up this new series of books about directors, so I proposed that we do it together. It was a little unusual having two people do one of them, but then I thought we should integrate the whole fact of it being a collaboration into the form of the book so that we'd write separate essays and then have conversations. Later on, we also did joint audio commentaries on home video releases of Kiarostami's *Close-Up*, *Life and Nothing More* and *The Wind Will Carry Us*.

You have worked on more collaborative books than any other critic I can think of.

Yes, four of my books are collaborations. With Hoberman there was *Midnight Movies*. There was also a book that has never come out in English, but came out in separate Italian and French versions, about Joe Dante and Roger Corman. I did this with Bill Krohn for the Locarno Film Festival when Marco Müller was the artistic director. They still owe me $1,000 for my work on that book, which included me buying my own air ticket to fly to Los Angeles. That was Marco's fault, because he exhausted his budget getting Tippi Hedren to come to the festival rather than paying me what I was owed according to our contract. He's always been apologetic about this, but I'm still pissed off about it.

Then there's *Movie Mutations*, started in collaboration with Kent Jones as co-editor, but then he suddenly backed out of it, apparently because his work as Martin Scorsese's ghostwriter was keeping him too busy, and I got Adrian Martin to take his place.

The book on Kiarostami with Mehrnaz was different from the other collaborations by being part of a series and having a partially predetermined format. But it was similar to *Midnight Movies* and *Movie Mutations* in combining individual essays with dialogues. And like *Movie Mutations*, it was explicitly multicultural. In fact, different sections of a dialogue that Mehrnaz and I had with Kiarostami in Chicago turned up in both books.

What drew you to Kiarostami's cinema?

I think it was his rather modernist disbelief in cinema as an institution, complicated and in some ways contradicted by his expertise at playing with cinematic conventions and codes as a master illusionist. Isn't it amazing that his oeuvre should end with the final clincher, the romantic kiss between the leads of *The Best Years of Our Lives*, in the last episode of his not-quite-finished *24 Frames*? Plus the young woman asleep at her computer on whose screen this kiss is seen by us but not by her. The fact that most of the actors in *A Taste of Cherry* never even met is a good illustration of Kiarostami's expert trickery, not to mention his grasp on reality versus pretense that enfolds every shot, whereas his imitators who aimed at neorealistic narratives never confused or challenged the reflexes of people like Roger Ebert. Those who compared Kiarostami to Vittorio De Sica or Satyajit Ray always missed the foundations of his cinema, which only pretended to be narratives in the conventional sense and, in fact, were much closer to being agnostic philosophical treatises disguised as stories. Most of Kiarostami's imitators phrase their films as statements; Kiarostami's are phrased as questions, explorations and journeys without clearly marked destinations or conclusions. For anyone who relies on the satisfying closures of conventional narratives, this can clearly be maddening.

I suspect that the only figure comparable to Kiarostami, both in terms of influence and in terms of stirring up controversies, would be Godard. Godard himself apparently once said that the cinema that begins with Griffith ends with Kiarostami. For me, both directors excelled in creating global newspapers during separate decades: Godard in the '60s, Kiarostami in the '90s. And people are still quarrelling about their formal procedures in comparable ways. Another parallel with Godard worth mentioning is the capacity of both filmmakers to keep reinventing themselves, in terms of audience, format, relation to narrative, and much else besides. You might even say that Godard and Kiarostami each have had as many "periods" as Picasso did.

I remember Mehrnaz disagreeing with me when I said Kiarostami was an intellectual. But even if he wasn't an intellectual by her definition, you wouldn't find many non-intellectual American filmmakers as interested in quoting writers like E.M. Cioran or referencing poets. Kiarostami's work is full of such references. That's one of the cultural differences that makes Iranian cinema so appealing. It has dimensions you wouldn't expect to find in American cinema.

I think part of it is that Kiarostami was very good at disguising himself behind this façade of being almost like a carpenter. To me, he was an extremely clever person—clever to the point of being an intellectual—who presented himself as a journeyman. His hobby was carpentry. That was part of the act.

I understand, and that's interesting. It reminds me of others who've done the same, like Jonas Mekas, who was also very clever at disguising himself in that way. Every time I would bring up Jacques Tati, Kiarostami would say, "Who is that? I've never heard of him." That was a total con game. Amir Naderi pointed out to me that Kiarostami had actually hung out with Tati when he was head of the jury at the Children's Film Festival in Tehran. For whatever reason—whether frivolous or serious—he didn't want me to compare him to Tati. But to me, there's a definite kinship there, if not an outright influence.

A House is Not a Home: Wright or Wrong

Is Mehrnaz's film A House is Not a Home: Wright or Wrong *close to what you might have envisioned as a film about your life and the Rosenbaum house designed by Frank Lloyd Wright?*

Yes and no. I did have some input on the film, but this was always input on *her* film, not mine or ours. For example, the title and subtitle were both suggested by me, but that was clearly based on what Mehrnaz's film was already saying, which had more to do with her family than it did with mine. It's true that ever since I saw *Last Year at Marienbad*, I had fantasies about tracking shots down the hallways of the house where I grew up. Then I had the idea of getting a wheelchair, as Raoul Coutard had done on Godard's *Breathless*, with me pushing Mehrnaz around as she filmed. A friend in Florence was kind enough to rent one for us. Those were my main contributions, apart from requesting that Mehrnaz add a sequence after I discovered that my brother Alvin had made a mistake in saying where a mezuzah belonged in relationship to the house's front door.* I said the reason for adding a sequence that mentioned this error wasn't to put Alvin down but to clarify how subjective all our memories were, that memory is always very selective and personal and it's the subjectivity that matters rather than any version of "the truth."

Mehrnaz readily agreed to shoot this sequence while finding many ways of making it her own, by selecting where we shot it, having me smoke a cigarette and read some of the opening passage in *Moving Places*—which I believe was her idea—and so on.

I also made a few suggestions to her about her short film *Jerry and Me*, but again, these were suggestions to implement her own ideas. For example, when she felt she was stuck for an ending, I proposed that she run through the entire film up to this point at a very fast speed to illustrate her dilemma. I also suggested that she needed to have at least some acknowledgment of the course she taught on Jerry Lewis and to show a little bit of it. So I was working as a kind of referee, I suppose—but a referee on her film, not mine.

Jerry Lewis

Did you ever have any encounters with Jerry Lewis?

Only one. And it was indirect. When he came to Chicago to appear in *Damn Yankees*, which I saw, one of his biggest fans in Chicago, a guy named Scott Marks, who taught at Columbia College, which is also where Mehrnaz teaches, arranged for him to do a Q&A with an audience. I went with Mehrnaz. It lasted for about three hours. I brought a copy of *Placing Movies* to give to him because of my piece on *Hardly Working* in it. Scott handed him the book backstage before the event, and reported back to me that Jerry Lewis started reading the piece and laughed out loud. So I can boast that I once made Jerry Lewis laugh! In the Q&A, I got him to talk about *Boy*, the last film he ever directed, a short that's rarely shown or seen. He was pleased that I mentioned it because he was very proud of it.

Have you seen the home movies that Jerry Lewis shot on 16mm, the remakes of famous films?

---

* A mezuzah is a small parchment containing specific verses from the Torah that is attached to the doorpost of a Jewish home.

I've seen pieces of them, including a few excerpts in Robert Benayoun's six-hour *Bonjour Mr. Lewis* and some other tributes. But yes, he came up with some great titles, like *Come Back, Little Shiksa*. I got to spend time with Janet Leigh, in both Cannes and Toronto, because of the *Touch of Evil* re-edit. She and Tony Curtis were neighbors and friends of Lewis, so she appeared in some of those films. I remember mentioning it to her, but it wasn't something she picked up on.

Why do you think Jerry Lewis is still, to this day, not recognized in America as one of the greatest American artists?

I think people are embarrassed by him and his movies because he reminds them of their awkwardness when they were young. The same reversal of attitude happened with Chaplin. Both men had cheering supporters who turned into lynch mobs. In the case of Jerry Lewis, the greatest kind of denial is not their outrage when they say, "Oh, the French like him," which by now has been out of date for almost half a century, but the fact that he was more popular in America than he ever could have been in France, when he and Dean Martin were making three films a year. *Sailor Beware* made more money than *The African Queen* or *On the Waterfront* or *Singin' in the Rain*. When you look at Serge Daney's writing about Jerry Lewis, he's seen as the embodiment of America. In *Which Way to the Front?*, Lewis plays an American tycoon called Byers who wants to enlist in the army but gets rejected by the draft, so he starts his own army. Serge said that his name sounds like "buyers," which is what Americans are, because America has a way of buying its way into the world community. Lewis was conveying all sorts of things about America, including the nouveau riche aspect. The point is that he put so much of himself up front that it became embarrassing to Americans that anybody could expose themselves that way. He makes up gags about his own open heart surgery and having wanted at one point to commit suicide. People aren't accustomed to the idea of comedians being that personal. He's also proud of his working-class origins, like Sam Fuller, which is the exact opposite of Woody Allen, who's ashamed of his background and reduces everything to middle-class reflexes.

Movie Mutations

Movie Mutations *was a major collaborative project that was eventually published as a book in 2003. Among the key contributors to the book is Adrian Martin. I understand that your relationship with him is somewhat strained at the moment, and it might be challenging for you to speak about him as objectively as possible.*

I first met Adrian when he wrote me a fan letter, enclosing some of his own writing, which included a lengthy essay about *Moving Places* and *Placing Movies* that he'd published in *Cinema Papers* and which I found very gratifying. Then we met in person in Melbourne shortly after I flew to Australia for the first time. I've been to that country three times now, and *Movie Mutations* initially grew out of a taped dialogue between us on one of those visits. Kent Jones was my original co-editor on the collection that grew out this, but Adrian gladly took over after Kent backed out, and I also enlisted Adrian to alternate with me as a columnist for the Spanish monthly film magazine *Caimán Cuadernos de Cine*.

    Adrian is obviously one of the best film critics we have, and possibly the most well-read in terms of his familiarity with other film critics. I especially like his 2014 book *Mise en Scène and Film Style*. The strain you refer to derives from him not considering me a friend anymore after I mentioned on some podcast that I thought he should write more and make fewer audiovisual essays. Both he and his Spanish partner unfriended me on social media, blocked me from accessing any of their posts on Twitter/X or Facebook or on her web site, and broke off all communications with me, all as a result of that one comment. For the life of me, I can't fathom why my opinion should matter so much; it makes me feel mythological when I'd rather be human and fallible. Adrian has the enthusiasm and the energy of a teenager but also some of a teenager's temperament.

Nicole Brenez is another figure associated with Movie Mutations, *and you dedicated one of your recent books,* Cinematic Encounters: Interviews and Dialogues, *to her.*

Nicole also reviewed *Moving Places* and *Placing Movies* together and I wanted to meet her as soon as I read her review. Her film taste is miles apart from mine, yet she's clearly a major and influential figure in terms of her originality, notably her theoretical writing about figuration, her versatility in terms of the kinds of cinema she writes about, and her rigor. I'm not the only one who considers her a goddess because of her extraordinary generosity, and I'm delighted that she was able to become one of Godard's key collaborators before he died.

Gilberto Perez

Another writer on film whom I discovered through your enthusiasm for his work is Gilberto Perez. What aspects of his writing resonate with you?

I became friends with the late Gil Perez as a direct result of my having selected an early essay of his about F.W. Murnau for my projected collection *Film Masters*, which never came out. His taste in film was quite distinct from mine, but his precision, which I assume partially came from his background as a nuclear physicist, was always impressive. I envied him for his ability to publish literary criticism as well as film criticism in literary publications. We were neighbors for a spell in Hoboken.

I've always thought of both Perez and Chris Fujiwara as examples of critics with a philosophical approach to film, writers whose every paragraph seems to grapple with a philosophical idea about the films they discuss. Does this interpretation of their work make sense to you?

I've never thought of Chris Fujiwara as a philosophical writer, although your question makes me feel that I should. I'm particularly taken with his books about Jacques Tourneur and Jerry Lewis, but I've also learned a lot from many of his shorter pieces.

As for Gil, his philosophical side may help to explain our conflicting tastes, such as his reverence for *The Deer Hunter*, a film I've always loathed. Even though our politics appeared to be similar, his investment in conservative films was something we often had friendly arguments about. I've never been able to figure out how much his Cuban background played a role in this. In many ways he seemed to me like an English liberal.

Festivals

Because your job at the Reader *was all about the city of Chicago, you didn't cover any foreign film festivals for the outlet, right?*

Well, not quite. The *Reader* did send me to—or at least allowed me to attend—the Toronto Film Festival, because that was a few weeks before the festival in Chicago, which allowed me to get a jump on that and various commercial releases.

There was also a year that I went to Cannes when the *Reader* asked me to take still photos and give a slide-show lecture, but they didn't "send" me to Cannes because I was already going there thanks to my four consecutive years on the New York Film Festival Selection Committee. So it's true that I didn't do any festival coverage except for the Chicago Film Festival. Then we tried to cover as many films as possible. But there wasn't any Toronto coverage per se in the *Reader*. I would just write about the Toronto films when they came to Chicago.

People who attend festivals often complain about the quality of the films, that they have to watch ten films in order to come across one or two titles that will be remembered the following year or even the following month. Do you think this is a new problem, or is it something you detected early on—that film festivals which last ten days generally can't find enough quality films to screen?

What's tricky about this is that even at the best film festivals, people tend to forget they're being selective. As I've already pointed out, nobody's in a position to know unless they've seen everything—and of course nobody has seen everything, so there's a certain amount of self-deception. In other words, it seems to me that there are different festival agendas. Cannes is mainly about the business, but at the same time, they get the first choice of what's thought to be artistically important. The question is whether you're seeing a film in order to judge it as a potential commercial release or if you're just sort of prospecting for a great work of art. If it's just consumer advice, then it's really not aesthetic criticism.

Festivals are different from each other. One that I've actually been to three times, which always amazes me, is the Melbourne Film Festival in Australia. Not once have I ever seen anybody take out a phone during a screening there. They just don't do it. And I noticed the one time I was at the film festival in Jeonju, South Korea, that they have an announcement asking people to stay to the end of the credits and then applaud. And people do it! It's a kind of formal politeness. All of which raises the issue of what the function of film criticism is.

You have been to film festivals under dictatorships—namely, San Sebastián under Franco and the Fajr Film Festival under the Islamic Republic regime. How do you navigate that? You know that the state has control over the festival, and at the same time you're there dealing with people who are passionate about cinema. How do you reconcile the fact of a state-sponsored event with the hope that you might discover valuable new work?

The one time I went to the San Sebastián Film Festival when Franco was in power, I lost my passport; it was stolen the last day I was at the festival. I had to stay in town for an additional night and take a bus to Bilbao to get to the American Consulate. I was actually glad that all happened because I was able to see things that the festival didn't want me to see, like the police station, for instance. I got to see a whole lot of Spain that I wouldn't have seen otherwise. One lasting memory of being there was reading the *New York Herald Tribune* with an entire article scissored out.

Did you experience a similar "fortunate" incident in Tehran?

The closest was a situation I had with Mehrnaz, whose U.S. passport expired while she was in Iran. She was told to get a replacement before coming back to the U.S., so I helped her find a U.S. embassy that could issue her a new passport.[*] We phoned various embassies in neighboring counties, and they were mostly sympathetic until they heard she was an Iranian dual national, and they backed off. She wound up having to go to Damascus on her Iranian passport, which meant she had to wait a whole extra week before she could fly home to the U.S. Mehnaz told me one of the embassy staff turned out to be an Abbas Kiarostami fan!

My favorite memory of that festival was a party given by Dariush Mehrjui, where Abbas Kiarostami smoked a home-grown joint with me, at his invitation, after Mehrnaz told him that I liked pot.

---

[*] There is no U.S. embassy in Tehran, which is why Mehrnaz and Jonathan had to contact embassies in neighboring countries.

I nominated Rakhshan Bani-Etemad to be head of the jury at Fajr, strictly as a polemical gesture, without knowing anything about her, and the other jurors agreed with me. Then I had another experience, which was hilarious: my friend Béla Tarr, who was also on the jury, hated everything being shown, so we couldn't reach a verdict at our final meeting because he kept vetoing every film. We'd been there all day and had hardly decided anything until he went to the men's room, at which point I made a quick proposal for all the prizes—basically honoring all the different biases of the other people on the jury, so that each person who liked a film could give it a prize—all before Béla came back from the bathroom. He wasn't angry at all; he was actually grateful that we were able to make progress with him out of the room.

It was Béla, by the way, who told me that Tehran reminded him of Budapest when it was still under Soviet control. It made him feel as if he was being constantly watched. That reminds me of the only time I ever spent in a Communist country, an afternoon in East Berlin the year before the Berlin Wall came down. Every bar and café I visited was eerily quiet, a silence I later understood was a safeguard against surveillance. Radu Jude's *Uppercase Print* (2020), adapted from a theater piece based on police records, deals potently with what that sort of life must have been like.

Jury Work

Is the social and collective aspect of working on a festival jury something that fascinates you?

Yes. I've even been a jury president a few times. I just had a reunion with a former fellow juror— Ralph McKay, a programmer living in Texas. It used to be that we never agreed about anything when we were both at Rotterdam or in New York. But then we both ended up on the jury of a film festival in Dallas, along with a woman who was a small-time Hollywood producer. She was so upset that the jury voted for a film that wasn't mainstream or Hollywood that she started calling him and me up in the middle of the night, trying to get us to change our votes. What was amazing is that suddenly, given that different context, Ralph and I agreed about everything. It's interesting how much a different context can cause you to change your position.

You told me you liked Rotterdam.

The first time I went there was because Jim Jarmusch and Sara Driver suggested to the festival director Huub Bals that he invite me, and after that I was invited every year while Huub was alive, whether I wrote something about the festival or not, which was incredible. I think one of the things that's interesting about Rotterdam is that they have a total commitment to experimental film, but their notion of experiment has more to do with content than style or form.

What about Russia?

I've been there only once. I was in Saint Petersburg for an international festival known as Message to Man. The jury deliberations became a battle of wills between me and someone I'd previously regarded as a friend, who actually walked out of the jury meeting because it wasn't going his way. We all had to sit around and wait for him to come back.

The last time I was at Mar del Plata there was someone on my jury who was a festival director himself. He was so angry that I was named the head of the jury instead of him that he wouldn't even deliberate with us. When another fellow juror of mine wrote her festival coverage, she didn't mention any of this, because the guy we were having trouble with was one of the best friends of her editor. There are all these complicated, hidden agendas that sometimes play roles that can be very annoying because they have so little to do with the art of cinema. People's egos often get so bound up in these things.

The marketing staff at film festivals today are as powerful as programmers.

Yes, and what's even worse is that there isn't much honesty about this, in terms of who has the power and how it's exerted. There's a whole lot that's unspoken, under the table. In other words, we all like to think that we have all the power. We didn't have it before. Do we have it now? It's certainly true that the availability of certain films all over the world online has changed the playing field quite a bit.

Orson Welles

When working full-time as a critic, did you have time for side projects? I'm trying to remember whether your work on Touch of Evil *overlapped with your time at the* Reader.

It overlapped. I first met Oja Kodar[*] when I was living in Santa Barbara and she invited me to edit *This Is Orson Welles* before I moved to Chicago, which is where I started that work, after I was mailed the audiotapes and manuscript by Bill Krohn, the critic and friend who first introduced me to Oja.

One thing about Oja that won me over was her telling me that the reason she wanted me to edit the book was her reactions to *Moving Places*, a copy of which I had given her. She said she needed an editor with a sense of poetry. It was indirectly from the Welles/Bogdanovich book that the *Touch of Evil* work arose. I had length restrictions from the publisher, and one way I adjusted to them was writing and publishing articles about Welles in magazines that derived from my research so that I could eliminate that material from the book and save space. "Orson Welles' Essay Films and Documentary Fictions" and "The Seven *Arkadins*," both included in my 2007 collection *Discovering Orson Welles*, grew out of that strategy.

Most of Welles' memo to Universal was part of the original manuscript that Craig Nelson—the HarperCollins editor on both *Midnight Movies* and *This is Orson Welles*—decided to delete for reasons of space (although we got him to restore it for the second edition), so I wound up getting it published in *Film Quarterly* and *Trafic* after *Film Comment* and *American Film* both rejected it. I was amazed that Richard Jameson, who was editing *Film Comment*, wasn't even curious enough to read the memo. His attitude was, "We've been running too much stuff about Welles lately."

Did you work on that project directly with Walter Murch?

Rick Schmidlin flew to Chicago and spent a weekend talking to me about it—that's how he got me involved. Walter Murch came on board afterwards, which was a brilliant move on Rick's part because Universal left us alone due to Walter's prestige. I would generally convey ideas to Rick, and he would pass them along to Walter. I also took

---

[*] Oja Kodar (b. 1941). Croatian sculptor, writer, actress and Orson Welles' partner and collaborator during the later years of his life.

the initiative of recording certain radio shows that I thought were relevant to the sound work and sending them to Walter. For example, Welles did an hour-long show called *Algiers*, based on the film *Algiers*.* The soundscapes seemed relevant to the soundtrack of the opening of *Touch of Evil*, which had been buried under the Henry Mancini music in earlier versions. The idea was to use music coming from various sources within the scene.

When we got to the rough cut, Rick sent me a video before finalizing it and asked for my input. I had two major objections. One was a mistake in the editing that Walter had made. There's an important moment in the film when Quinlan is heard off-screen hitting a Mexican suspect in the stomach while trying to get a confession. That had been cut out in the studio release but was still present in the preview version. I insisted it had to be restored because it was a major addition, and Walter agreed.

The second issue was about crosscutting. Welles' memo specified that the two narrative strands after the explosion—one involving Charlton Heston, the other involving Janet Leigh—should be given equal weight in the cutting. Murch did more back-and-forth cutting than Welles requested, making it feel like standard TV crosscutting rather than two extended stretches of action. I argued that it didn't adhere to what Welles requested in the memo. Rick decided to sleep on it, and the next morning, he agreed with me and overruled Walter.

I remember being assigned to write about the project for its premiere. I called Janet Leigh for an interview. Interestingly, I was told she would call me, not the other way around. We arranged a time, but then she didn't call. I figured she couldn't be bothered, but the next day, she left me a long voicemail apologizing profusely and giving me her number to call anytime. I did, and that's how we became friends.

With Walter Murch, it took me almost a full day to reach him for the same article. He didn't return my calls, and I think it might have been because he was used to being the only intellectual on a project. He also might have felt uneasy or annoyed after I'd critiqued his work on another picture, Robert Duvall's *The Apostle*. I had seen it at Toronto and loved it, but he had cut out parts I admired. Apparently, someone at *Variety* suggested the film would be better if trimmed by 30 minutes, and that led to his edits. I found it

---

* A 1938 Walter Wanger production, directed by John Cromwell, and conceived as a remake of *Pépé le Moko*.

troubling that someone could step in after one viewing and dictate cuts to a director who had worked on the film for months or years. Murch wasn't hostile to me, but I think I made him uncomfortable.

When did you watch the restored version of Touch of Evil *for the first time with an audience? At Cannes?*

It wasn't at Cannes because the screening there was canceled. We were all there, but Beatrice Welles threatened a lawsuit because they hadn't paid her any money. It was ridiculous because she didn't have any rights, but that was her way of getting attention. Toronto may have been the first time I saw it, but it's more likely that it was at the film festival in Turin.

Twice I got to spend an entire day with Janet Leigh— once driving around the Côte d'Azur with her in a limo and then being her dinner escort, and another time in Toronto when we were doing press for the film. I'd had such a huge crush on her as a child that it was wonderful hanging out with her and discovering how sharp and thoughtful she was.

By the way, apart from *The Stranger*, I believe that the *Touch of Evil* re-edit was the only Welles-directed release that ever turned a profit.

Did you ever get hold of the complete memo?

Oh, that's an amazing story! I only had two-thirds of the memo when we started work. Universal didn't have the whole document, but I knew Charlton Heston had a copy because, when I published two-thirds of it in *Film Quarterly*, he saw it, wrote me a nice letter, and said, "I still remember that memo because I have a copy in my files." When we needed the full memo, I told them to go to Heston. They didn't want to approach him directly and had to find an intermediary, which seemed crazy to me. I think it might have been Lew Wasserman whom they asked to help. Eventually, they got the full memo, and I asked if they could send me a copy. They hesitated, but finally agreed on the condition that I sign a document swearing not to reveal its existence to anyone. I signed it, of course, even though by then I had already published most of it in two separate languages, in both *Film Quarterly* and *Trafic*. This kind of insanity happens in studios when people in these situations know very little but are terrified of upsetting their bosses.

You mentioned encountering similar challenges when working on The Other Side of the Wind.

Yes, but that was different, and with a less happy outcome. In that case, it was about the sound edit of the film. Most of the people working on it were Hollywood veterans, but *The Other Side of the Wind* is not a Hollywood film—it's anti-Hollywood. The editing and sound design shouldn't feel like a Hollywood picture, but they insisted on doing it that way despite my objections as a consultant. The gay-baiting scene with John Huston and Dan Tobin was a lot creepier and far more confrontational before they added the offscreen tinkling of a piano in another room for some stupid reason. I think they weakened the sequence considerably by insisting on pointless continuity.

What are your thoughts on The Other Side of the Wind *now, in hindsight?*

There are two issues: the film as it was edited and the film apart from that. Some of Welles' ideas clearly weren't carried out. He wanted the material from the film-within-the-film and the party scenes to have equal length and prominence. But almost everyone involved, including Welles experts like Joe McBride, wanted the party scenes to dominate.

The film-within-the-film confused people, including me at first. Welles' and Kodar's idea was that Oja was playing the role of John Huston in the film-within-the-film, representing someone attracted to his leading man but expressing it by sleeping with his leading lady. That concept doesn't come across clearly; it feels strange and registers as mannerist.

That said, *The Other Side of the Wind* is certainly Welles' most experimental film. What's most off-putting is that it's a very bitter film. Another problematic aspect is that the character Huston plays doesn't seem even remotely like the kind of person who would make the film-within-the-film. It's just not believable. I know that Welles often portrayed human personality as an enigma. He exploited these contradictions throughout his career, going all the way back to *Citizen Kane*, but I'm not sure this contradiction works here.

I consider *Don Quixote* Welles' most important unfinished work—more significant than *The Other Side of the Wind*. After years of pestering Oja, Catherine Benamou, Esteve Riambau, former head of the Filmoteca de Catalunya in Barcelona, and I finally convinced her to let an archive preserve it, ideally the Filmoteca Española in Madrid. Esteve is leading a research effort to inventory what's already available in Madrid, Paris, and Rome. So, hopefully, eventually, we'll see what there is of it.

I think more highly of *The Other Side of the Wind* than most people do, but I also don't think we're ready for it yet. Parts of it fascinate me. For instance, in the party scenes, you almost never see any couples, even though the film-within-the-film is exclusively about a couple. I don't know if that was intentional on Welles' part, but it's intriguing.

It's a very interesting film, but it rubs people the wrong way. Even though it's anti-Hollywood, it doesn't establish its own form of coherence. It's still somewhat incoherent, and it may be too early to know if time will change that. But, meanwhile, I'm angry that Criterion has refused to bring it out on DVD or Blu-ray. They have an exclusive deal with Netflix, so apparently if they don't release it, no one else can. One original plan was to include as an extra Welles' edit of the long sex sequence in the car in its complete form, because they shortened it in the version shown on Netflix. Maybe I'm wrong about this, but I'm guessing that Criterion passed on the film because of its political incorrectness—Oja playing a Native American—though Charlton Heston playing a Mexican in *Touch of Evil* is deemed okay now. Time always changes what is or isn't acceptable, and it seems shortsighted to subject a Welles film to this kind of capitalist suppression.

What did you think of Netflix editing the Dennis Hopper footage and adding "Directed by Orson Welles" to it?*

Criminal and obnoxious. They flew me out to spend an afternoon talking to the main editor of *The Other Side of the Wind*, Bob Murawski. Joe McBride and I were shown a rough cut together. Bob agreed with several of my arguments. For example, I hate the music in *The Other Side of the Wind*. It's utterly dreadful. I think it was the last thing Michel Legrand did before he died. In an interview, he said, "I'm so happy to have done this score because it's my homage to Orson," but his homage wasn't what the film needed. The issue is that Welles had significant editorial control over how he used Legrand's music in *F for Fake*, but that control was absent here. In fact, I think one of the film's biggest flaws is the soundtrack.

---

* This morally questionable Netflix product was shown in 2020 as *Hopper/Welles*.

In The Other Side of the Wind, *I was expecting to hear some sort of rock soundtrack, because of the reference to* Zabriskie Point *and the time period.*

I think Welles started out with the idea of doing a parody of *Zabriskie Point* and then went off in another direction. Throughout his career, he would take characters or concepts—sometimes ones he was completely opposed to, like Hank Quinlan—and try to make them as sympathetic as possible. Similarly, when he was supposedly making a parody of Antonioni, I think he actually got into an arty style. Oja had almost no sense of Antonioni's style, and I believe her when she says she directed two or three sequences in the film-within-the-film. People assume she's tooting her own horn when she talks about her involvement, but it's just the opposite. She's never even seen the whole film in its final state because her relationship to it has been so traumatic. It represented so many years of constant struggle and frustration for her.

I've often said that one thing she and Welles had in common was that they were both reclusive exhibitionists. That sounds like a total paradox, but I think it's true for both of them. And part of Welles' exhibitionism was expressed through her exhibitionism in some fashion.

Welles claimed that the film wasn't autobiographical, but of course it is. You can't see it any other way. It even plays with the idea of the audience interpreting it as autobiographical.

John Huston

What do you think of Huston as a director?

I have nothing but admiration for *Wise Blood*. *The Dead* is pretty amazing, too. And there are others, like *The Man Who Would Be King*. He was an intellectual and a literary person, both qualities that I see as definite pluses. But he was also a sadist, and that sadism often gets in the way for me. And his brand of macho doesn't appeal to me either.

That's partly why I have trouble appreciating filmmakers like Losey and Pinter. There's a lot of sadomasochism in their work. One of my problems with Fassbinder, for instance, is that his films always feel like a tug-of-war between Marxism and sadism, and of course the sadism always wins. Anytime there's a conflict between sadism and Marxism—or between sadism any other -ism—sadism tends to dominate because people respond to the dynamics of power more than they'd care to admit. Trump's triumph in the recent election seems to confirm that. Zadie Smith's recent suggestion that Trump may only be Elon Musk's Trojan horse seems even more relevant. The so-called consensus appears to be not only that the robber barons are the ones in charge but that they should be. That's part of my problem with Huston. Plus, he was complicit in making so many lousy movies.

Chicago Reader II

Were there any disadvantages to having a steady job as a critic for the Reader?

The main one for me was living in Chicago, because I'd been spoiled by having lived in New York and Paris. That, for me, is significant in all kinds of ways—not just in terms of what's available culturally, but also because, to really make it in New York, you have to be in New York. I'm envious of someone like A.S. Hamrah because the current issue of the *New York Review of Books* has him reviewing a film. All my attempts to write for them have failed, even though I came close a couple of times. Part of this has to do with the attitude in New York that if it hasn't happened there, it hasn't happened.

At the *Reader*, the only disadvantages I noticed at first were interpersonal. I never became close friends with anyone there. It was always a working relationship, never a friendship. I would have liked to have developed friendships there. I remember asking a couple of the women on the *Reader* staff to accompany me to the opening night of the Chicago Film Festival, just after I started the job, and they both turned me down. But for at least the first ten years, my isolation didn't matter so much.

If you see living in Chicago as an obstacle, why didn't you move somewhere else after retiring from the Reader *sixteen years ago?*

The main reason was all my possessions, including my condo that I purchased in 1998—the only time in my life I've ever owned property. Selling all my DVDs will lighten the load a bit, but I still have an enormous number of books. Moving anywhere else would cost a lot of money, and I don't have a lot of money.

When I left New York, I felt like I was being run out of town because I'd been outspoken in criticizing a few other critics. Some people wouldn't even speak to me. One thing I like about Chicago, compared to New York, is how socially relaxed it is, whereas, generally, I found the atmosphere in New York poisonous—and still do, to a certain extent. But I still miss New York.

What is your absolute favorite city in the world to live in?

Paris.

After Paris?

New York. But I also love Vienna and Buenos Aires.

How long did it take for this experience to become frustrating, having to review so many films you wouldn't normally choose to watch?

I'm not sure, but it gradually crept up on me, like a fungus or a virus, which had also happened at *Monthly Film Bulletin*.

So you thought of retiring from the Chicago Reader?

It had to do with several factors, but mainly with the gradual erosion of what made my position at the *Chicago Reader* unique. Almost every privilege I had there disappeared, one by one.

Having an unlimited word count was a big deal, but over time that perk was taken away. In the beginning, I could write about any film playing in Chicago, no matter what it was or when it had premiered. That changed, and I was restricted to reviewing films only the week they opened. The job started to feel more and more like everywhere else.

One key moment stands out, which I've never fully acknowledged. When the editors decided I needed a "second stringer" to share the workload, I was hopeful. They advertised the position and received a lot of applications. I reviewed those applications and had someone in mind—a local person I thought would be great. But they ignored my input entirely and instead assigned the job to someone already on staff, a music critic with no real background in film. That decision reflected how the *Reader* was beginning to operate like other publications in ways I didn't approve of. The fact that I'd been hired because I knew about film was very unusual and was really because of Dave Kehr. This rarely happens in the United States. In fact, it's usually counted against you because there's a worry that you'll be too esoteric. That's probably also why Dave was not hired to replace Janet Maslin at *The New York Times*.

During that same period, the *Reader* transitioned from being a writer-focused paper to an editor-focused one. At the start of my tenure, the environment was much freer and more collaborative. Early on, many of the *Reader* editors were also writers. Later, they stopped writing entirely or did so very rarely. This change contributed to the *Reader* losing some of its unique identity. Alison True, who edited the *Reader* for most of my tenure, believed that *every* piece had to be edited, even if it was excellent as submitted. Her philosophy was that editing always made a piece better. I disagreed and saw this policy as demoralizing to writers, at least in the long run. When I worked for *Sight and Sound*, Penelope Houston didn't take that approach. She believed there was value in pieces so well written that they required no editing.

Over time, this relentless editing process became depressing, even though the editors were very skilled. The silver lining was that they helped make my work more comprehensible to a broader audience. The editors weren't cinephiles, so they pushed me to write in a way that a general audience could understand, even if they weren't particularly interested in film. I miss that kind of feedback today.

For example, I've been working on my book, *Camera Moments That Confound Us*. It's a very eccentric book, and I've worried that it might be seen as too unconventional. I recently wrote to the publisher to check on its status, and they assured me it's with some readers now. But not having the sort of immediate feedback I used to get from the *Reader* makes things harder. More generally, the differences between writing for a weekly and writing for a book are enormous and require some adjustments.

One of the *Reader*'s strengths had always been its political writers. These people were among the first to be made redundant when there were budget cuts. If you decide to go mainstream and compete with *Time* magazine, you're bound to lose, meanwhile removing most of the reasons why the *Reader* existed. They ran a feature called "What the *Reader*'s reading," and once their recommendations became exclusively mainstream, I thought they were promoting their own demise. I guess I was wrong, because they still exist, but I barely mind the fact that I have trouble finding the paper these days in my own neighborhood.

Also, for the first ten years or so, I worked on the main floor with the rest of the staff. Then they moved me upstairs, to a quieter area where only a few people worked on layout and similar tasks. It felt isolating—almost like being treated as an outsider, a leper even.

So you just handed in your resignation, and that was the end of it at the Chicago Reader?

When I mentioned to Alison that I was planning to retire, she didn't want me to go. If not the most popular writer at the *Reader*, I was certainly near the top, and a lot of people read the paper specifically because of me. Alison offered to make things easier for me, proposing to lighten certain aspects of the workload that I found less appealing. She didn't mention a raise, as I recall, but her proposals didn't carry much weight because I'd already made up my mind.

My views often clashed with the editors. Over time, the alienation grew, both on my side and theirs. Most of the resentment tended to be passive-aggressive. For example, when I wrote in one column that George W. Bush had wanted to invade Iraq even before the Gulf War, Alison assigned a writer to research and essentially try to debunk me.

There were other moments that highlighted this tension. Alison had hired a second-string film critic for the *Reader*—Lisa Alspecter—who was, to put it mildly, not very knowledgeable about film history. Her biggest calling card was probably her eccentricity. She once wrote a defense of Gus Van Sant's *Psycho* remake, comparing it to doing different productions of a Shakespeare play. That argument upset me so much that I wrote a lengthy rebuttal, which the *Reader* published.

Another instance that irked me was when I wrote a scathing capsule review of the remake of *The Manchurian Candidate*, which I found appalling. That same writer who was enlisted to debunk me gave it a four-star review that wasn't very convincing. As I recall, he hadn't even seen the original, and I was told later that he did it largely to undermine my status and challenge my taste, not because he was all that enthusiastic about the movie. Tragically, this writer had personal struggles and eventually committed suicide.

Financially, things were shifting too. Thanks to the *Reader*'s excellent profit-sharing system, I had accumulated enough money to buy a condo. But my decision to retire wasn't about money at all. I simply felt it was time. Most critics don't stay in the field as long as I had, and many eventually burn out. I wasn't necessarily burned out yet, but I could see it coming. I knew that if I didn't quit soon,

I risked becoming a less interesting writer and losing my enjoyment of the work. It felt like the right moment to leave, to ensure I left on a high note rather than overstaying my welcome.

In some ways, I miss my job at the *Reader*. Having that kind of platform and audience was amazing. Even today, I'll meet people in Chicago who want to take selfies with me or treat me like a minor celebrity, which is flattering and a bit surreal.

You quit in 2008?

That's right. The date I set for quitting was right after my 65th birthday.

Going Online

My introduction to your work came after you left the Reader. *Suddenly you became more international, thanks to the Internet and your website.*

I owe everything to the *Reader* for putting my work online. When they launched their website, they not only uploaded current pieces but also all of my earlier work for them, although they didn't go far back enough to include the long reviews by Dave Kehr, which I always found unfortunate. I think that omission partly explains why Dave eventually gave up film criticism altogether.

How long after that did you start your own website, jonathanrosenbaum.com?

It wasn't exactly started by me. Before I quit, the *Reader* had been bought by a company called Creative Loafing. They approached me and said, "Since you're leaving the *Reader*, would you like to have a website?" At the time, I was just getting started with all this stuff, and I wasn't even sure I wanted a website. That's how little I knew—I was very skeptical and more than a little naïve about the Internet. So I said, "Okay, but only if I can have total editorial control." Alison didn't want me to have that; she wanted some kind of veto or editorial oversight. But I won—they decided to go with my preferences. I owe everything to Creative Loafing, even though they later went bankrupt.

At first, the website was on the *Reader*'s server as jonathanrosenbaum.com. Eventually, a guy from Australia named Rowan McNaught, a professional website designer, proposed redesigning the site, free of charge, and did a fantastic job. Then, after a certain point, I decided to shift to another server. Rowan set it up with an Australian company that still manages the site, which became jonathanrosenbaum.net.

What was amazing is I never had any contract with the *Reader*. Everything was on a handshake basis. Technically, they still own everything I ever wrote for them. But over time, they became too preoccupied with other things, so they let me handle reprints and even pocket most of the money made from them.

They always edited me, but if I go back to a piece I published in the Reader and don't like the way it was edited, I can post my original draft instead. I've done that in a few cases.

Before I moved the website with Rowan's help, the large company that bought the *Reader* felt like a Hollywood office. I'd wait for an hour or two just to see the publisher, and the meeting would last five minutes because they were so busy. At a certain point, I realized I didn't even need their permission to move the website—they had never even visited it! So we just moved it all to the new server, and it worked out.

It was a step-by-step process, where I became independent of the *Reader*. After I left, they asked me to shorten some of my capsule reviews when they started to have length issues, so sometimes there are two versions of the same capsule on my website—one longer, one shorter—but I've never systematically fixed that.

For most of my website's existence, I would publicize it two or three times a day on Facebook and Twitter/X. Now, I preset everything because I've gotten so busy with other things. I don't check how many people visit or if my Google Analytics is working properly. I've averaged about a thousand visitors a day for a long time, so I figure that'll continue.

These days, my relationship with my website is more casual. Once I preset what's going to be posted, I'm done with it. Only very occasionally do I publicize posts.

Back to Print

Does this casualness have something to do with the fact that, in a way, you have gone back to print media? With all the books you have produced, in a way you're actually doing what you wanted to do pre-digital.

That is partly true. It's funny... I'm in correspondence with a friend, Nick Macdonald, who has been working on an ambitious book for years. It's about film and death—depictions of death and attitudes towards it. He's going through almost the entire history of cinema, writing about individual films.

He wanted advice about publishers, and I suggested Hat and Beard Press, my own publisher for *In Dreams Begin Responsibilities*. He just responded, saying they charge an awful lot for their books and wondering why I don't go with a more mainstream publisher. He doesn't understand that, while I may be a familiar name in hardcore cinephile circles, I'm not well known outside of that.

My last experiences with mainstream publishers were frustrating. *In Dreams Begin Responsibilities* was rejected by two academic presses—not by the editors, but by their publicists. It's funny because my most successful solo book, *Movie Wars*, was published by a very small Chicago press, yet it became my best seller.

I had tried to get Farrar, Strauss and Giroux interested in the same project. An editor there went to bat for it, but the publisher ultimately turned it down. So, the mainstream press has never really been an option for me. At least, my assumption is that they wouldn't want to publish my books.

I know you because of your website, and it means a great deal to me. But after all these years, what, in your opinion, is the negative side, if any, of publishing online?

The fact that I publish books, even ones that mainly consist of material already available on my website, shows my feeling that publishing online isn't enough. The writing that matters most to me is something I want to have in book form, not just on the Internet. I suppose that's a kind of negative view of online publishing, but it's also a defense of literature.

I deliberately used an email account I don't check often as my contact address for the website. That way, if I get a message sent to that account, I know it came through the website. I wanted to keep the website in a separate category from the books of mine sitting on a shelf. It's like I have two audiences: one that reads me through books, probably an older audience, and one that follows me online.

And the narrative you create by putting together your essays in book form is something that's very difficult to reproduce on a website?

Yes, absolutely. One important thing about *In Dreams Begin Responsibilities* is that it changed my perception of my own work. I realized I had been writing about connections between literature, jazz and film from the very beginning. It runs through all my work, but I hadn't noticed how much until I assembled the book.

The process of putting together *In Dreams Begin Responsibilities* reshaped my view of individual pieces. It also reminded me how important music and literature have been to me since I was very young. Books allow me to reshape my oeuvre and redefine its significance. That control is essential to me. When I was writing for the *Reader*, the publication was designed to be read for a week and then forgotten, like all the other free weeklies. Books exist on a much longer timeline compared to the ephemeral nature of weekly publications.

CRITIC AS ARTIST

Did you manage to write your review of Megalopolis?

Yes. It's posted on the BFI's website, and will be printed in the next issue of the magazine. They ran it online earlier because the film opens in the U.K. today.*

I'm going to see it on Monday. I wonder what you thought of the film.

It's a very mixed bag. I consider it a failure artistically, but it's very daring. It qualifies in some ways as an experimental film—but not always in a good way; it's often very confusing. The theme of my review is that Coppola is somebody obsessed with revising his self-portraits. And this is, of course, one of his self-portraits, like many others, but his whole career has been about revising himself, even when it gets down to whether he calls himself Francis Coppola or Francis Ford Coppola. And I discuss the relation of the new film to other films that he's either distributed or made himself. As much as I'm impressed by *Apocalypse Now*, I'm really offended by the fact that it's a film about the war in Vietnam without the Vietnamese, because it was shot in the Philippines and uses Filipino peasants to represent Vietnamese peasants. I mean, there's not even any visible curiosity about the Vietnamese.

Basically, Coppola's best films are often about powerful men, seen as self-portraits. I think that's both the strength and the limitation of this film. He's one of the only people who seems equally invested in being a kind of businessman and being an artist. Sometimes people fuse—or, rather, confuse—these two functions into some imaginary version of consensus, but I believe they're more often likely to be in conflict.

Video Essay

We worked together on some video essays about Dreyer and Béla Tarr.† What are your thoughts on the potential and limitations of the audiovisual format as a tool for criticism?

---

* You can find this piece under the title "*Megalopolis* Second Look Review" (27 September 2024). I'm reluctant to paste the website link here as these days who types an entire address line into the search tab? We all Google things, don't we?

† I produced these two videos for BBC Persian in London. I was approached by BBC because they had unused archive interviews with the filmmakers in question and didn't know what to do with them. In both cases, Jonathan wrote the text and appeared in the video, Mehrnaz Saeed-Vafa handled the filming, and I produced and edited the work.

I've also made several video essays with Kevin Lee, but most of those that I've done with both of you are essentially illustrations of ideas I already broached in my writing. The two exceptions to this that come to mind are the two-part video I did with Kevin comparing *The Sun Shines Bright* and *Gertrud* and one on *Out 1* that was largely built around Kevin's visual ideas. Kevin is a real master of this form. I'm wary of generalizing about print criticism versus video criticism because I see the latter as primarily the domain of you, Mehrnaz and Kevin, rather than mine.

Critic as Teacher

Which of the courses you've taught in recent years have best allowed you to connect with students?

Maybe when I taught a series of courses at the School of the Art Institute, with screenings and lectures also open to the public, based on different decades—like World Cinema of the '30s, '40s, '50s and '60s. I had courses that I taught about each one. I think I was at my best doing that or else showing and discussing some of my favorite films at Béla Tarr's film.factory in Sarajevo. I was somehow able to communicate. One example is when I was doing World Cinema of the '60s, one of the films I showed was William Klein's *Mr. Freedom*. Of course, I would be writing capsule reviews in the *Reader* for the same films that were showing because those classes were open to the public. I wrote in my capsule review of *Mr. Freedom* that it may be the most anti-American movie ever made. Apparently as a result of my writing that, we had turnaway crowds. It was almost like people who probably didn't even think they were anti-patriotic were really curious. Somehow I was speaking to that constituency, and that was very pleasing to me.

Where was this?

In Chicago, at the Gene Siskel Film Center.

Béla Tarr's film.factory

How did your teaching at film.factory come about?

When I met Béla at a festival, I discovered that he really liked an article of mine about his films *Almanac of Fall* and *Damnation* called "A Bluffer's Guide to Béla Tarr."

The idea behind the piece was that you didn't need to be an expert in Hungarian cinema to engage with his work. I also poked fun at some interpretations. For example, I noted that people claimed his roving camera symbolized a desire to escape from Communism. Tarr liked that observation because he found such readings farfetched. He often disagreed adamantly with critics, including me. For example, he rejected the idea that *Sátántangó* had anything to do with Hungary's political situation, despite the novel being written under Soviet control and the film being made after that. He viewed his themes as timeless, not as political statements.

We became friends, spending more time together when he visited Chicago. I was on the New York Film Festival selection committee and advocated for *Sátántangó*. I later chose it as a critic's choice for the Chicago Film Festival.

At the Toronto festival, I urged my colleagues to attend the press screening of *Sátántangó*, but almost nobody showed up. Yet the public screening was packed and the audience stayed through the entire film. That was significant to me; it reinforced my belief that the public is often ahead of critics in terms of sophistication.

In fact, I quit the Chicago Critics Association for this reason. When it came to choosing the best foreign film, most critics had seen very few candidates—only ones heavily promoted in Chicago. The public often selected more interesting films. I felt that by staying in the organization, I was complicit in lowering rather than raising public standards, since the critics were less discerning. I haven't regretted leaving.

Jim Hoberman and I were both invited to a film festival in Poland where they were showing *The Turin Horse*, in addition to various midnight movies. (A former student of Jim's had just translated our book into Polish.) This was when Béla announced that it was his last film. I managed to get an assignment to write about *The Turin Horse* for *Film Comment*. Béla was there, and I hadn't seen him in a good while. He told me about this film school he wanted to start and asked me if I could become involved. I said, "Sure, I'd love to be."

At first, he thought it was going to be located in Split in Croatia rather than in Sarajevo, but they ran into various technical problems about state funding and things of this kind. Eventually, when they wound up going to Sarajevo, I went there. I think I've said before that I consider it not only the best place I've ever taught at, but the best educational institution I've ever been associated with.

It was very intense and very relaxed, with very gifted students handpicked by Béla, and even though they all worked on each other's films, there was no sense of competitiveness among them, or at least none that I could see. It was sort of like working independently of the people who were paying the money to allow it to go on, to exist. Béla is not a person who ever compromises on anything.

Béla didn't think of it as a school but as what the name suggested: a factory for making films. He didn't care about the rest, and wouldn't play ball with requests for having certain formal requirements met. During the time I was there, they wouldn't take attendance. People would come to class if they wanted to, but there wasn't any policing of them or giving them grades or anything like that. Finally the donors withdrew their support and the school came to an end. He wanted to have it start up again elsewhere, but partly because of his health issues, which meant he was spending more time in Budapest with his doctors, it hasn't happened. Even though he serves on juries at festivals, he doesn't want to make films again.

I haven't been in touch with him much since the school closed. Most of the news I have about Béla comes from Sunčica Fradelič, who basically ran the office at film.factory. She's a good friend who runs a little film organization in Split and has hired me to do various gigs there.

Tell me of your teaching methodology at the school.

Pretty simple. Basically, I'd show them a film and then we'd discuss it. But we'd discuss it not only in class but over meals, and I'd hang out with them. We'd also go to hear jazz together at local clubs. When I got there, the first semester I went, they usually had only two guests teaching at one time. One would do something related to history and criticism, and the other would be a filmmaker.

The filmmaker when I went the first time was Carlos Reygadas. He had to leave early, or our schedules didn't quite coincide, so I ended up spending a lot of extra time teaching. I even started scheduling weekend sessions at an apartment that several students shared. Béla eventually said, "Look, you're taking the students away from their own work," in terms of the films they were making, and he asked me to spend less time teaching.

I stayed in what was generally regarded as the best hotel in Sarajevo, only five minutes from film.factory, which was on the campus of an existing university, although it was separate from their film department. I have extremely fond memories of the time I spent there. Sarajevo was a wonderful city, even after a devastating war. There's even a square named after Susan Sontag, who loved the place so much she kept coming back.

In the evenings, I often had dinner with Béla and the other guests. I got to hang out with Tilda Swinton, for example. Once or twice, I combined my visit to Sarajevo with trips to visit Oja Kodar in Croatia. One time, when I didn't get confirmation about a visit to Oja, I stayed in Sarajevo for a few extra days. I attended lectures on acting by Tilda Swinton, which was a mind-boggling experience These lecture demonstrations involved her videotaping the students and me, commenting on the tapes, and directing us to react certain ways in close-ups. It was a really extraordinary experience. I'm sorry I wasn't able to continue beyond the few years that film.factory existed.

One thing I discovered just a couple of days ago was a bunch of DVDs of work by students who had given me their films. I was glad I hadn't lost them and that they hadn't made it into the registry of the things I sold.

Critic as Curator

Some critics have taken the direction of curating and programming as a new tool of critical engagement. Have you ever considered that?

Whenever I teach, it's sort of curating. And you know, I enjoy teaching a lot, but, as with my writing, I'm very much at the mercy of people when they want something from me.

Have you ever curated any extended series for cinematheques, festivals, and repertory cinemas?

I did "The Unquiet American: Transgressive Comedies from the U.S." for the Viennale and the Austrian Film Archives, a month-long series with a book-length catalogue in 2009, which is probably the most elaborate retrospective I've curated, apart from "Rivette in Context" for London's National Film Theatre and New York's Bleecker Street Cinema in the late 1970s.

At the Gene Siskel Film Center, run by the School of the Art Institute, I've taught many courses that doubled as weekly film programs, and always enjoy my lectures/discussions, enhanced by the perk that a teaching assistant grades student papers. Many of these courses were devoted to world cinema in separate decades, and I also taught courses there on Orson Welles and Agnès Varda. I've also done week-long screening-and-lecture series on Welles, Stroheim and Tati at the Cinemateca Portuguesa in Lisbon, and hope to do one there on Jacques Tourneur.

I don't think critics should ever have the first or last word on any film, but they should improve the level of the discussion in some way, and that's what I try to do. Of course, programming a film means endorsing it in some fashion, but the audience isn't obliged to agree. The discussion begins before the critic comes along and continues after the critic leaves.

It does seem to me that people who make films about film are also curators. And, of course, I've worked with people who are doing that.

Am I right to think conversation is, for you, a format that you appreciate a lot in filmmaking? In other words, films that are based on conversations between people.

Sure. I wrote an essay about a Japanese film called 2/*Duo*, directed by Nobuhiro Suwa, which was shot by a very interesting cinematographer, Masaki Tamura, who has a unique way of filming conversations and discussions which sometimes privileges the listeners rather than the speakers. He shot a series of documentaries about protests against the building of Tokyo's Narita airport, trying to change the power dynamics in those discussions. Also, *Jazz on a Summer's Day* is as much about listening to jazz as it is about performing jazz. It's possibly the best jazz film about listening, although there are other great ones about the audience, like the beginning of Ingmar Bergman's film of *The Magic Flute*.

A Day in the Life of JR

What does a typical day in your life look like?

Lately, I've been going to sleep much earlier than I used to. But on most days the order in which I do things is very much improvised. I have to write a reader's report now for a manuscript that's almost a thousand pages long. It's hard for me to discipline myself to sit down and do nothing but that. I often do several things at once, shifting from one to the other according to how I'm feeling at the moment. It's very much a free-form improvisation.

Do you watch films on a daily basis?

I start to watch them, but these days, after having to see all of everything when I wrote for the BFI and the *Reader*, I get impatient. While preparing to see *Megalopolis*, I thought, "Okay, I should probably start thinking about Coppola and look at one of his films, " so I decided to watch *Rumble Fish* again last night. It was kind of interesting but I didn't get very far. He's trying to make an art film for a teenage market. But at the same time, I tend to see Coppola as a mannerist, not as a stylist, because he takes on a manner the way that somebody tries on a different suit of clothes to see how it looks. And to me, that's a limiting factor about him as a filmmaker.

It also has to do with the fact that almost all of the book I just finished writing was written while being stoned on liquid marijuana, more precisely on Delta 8 tincture, which I ingest now with an eye dropper. Generally I revise when I'm not stoned. But being stoned on my first drafts makes it more of an unblocked improvisation.

Going to the Movies

How often do you go to the cinema now?

More often than once a month, less often than once a week.

Aside from the social interaction, what's the difference for you between watching films at home, in a cinema, or at a film festival?

One major discovery I've made over the years is that I basically see film as a social activity. Even if you're watching something alone at home on your laptop, it's still a social activity because inevitably you end up discussing it with other people, on the Internet or elsewhere. It's kind of funny, because I grew up in a small town in Alabama, and it wasn't like I thought that I necessarily had a certain kinship with the other people who were seeing the films that I saw. But most of the people who read me religiously are not people in Alabama. As James Naremore has written, part of my work has been creating bridges between different parts of my life that were previously disconnected. For example, before I wrote *Moving Places*, the fact that I grew up in a family of movie exhibitors and the fact that I later became a film critic were not connected.

Home Video

When did you buy your first VCR, and how much was your thinking on film shaped by your ability to rewatch and closely examine films on VHS, and later on DVD and Blu-ray?

I'm terrible when it comes to dates, but my introduction to the second edition of *Moving Places* quotes from a commissioned article I wrote on this subject in 1979, before I owned a VCR of my own. If I'd had a VCR in the 1970s, I couldn't or wouldn't have written *Moving Places*, at least not in the same way.

I don't think that videos, DVDs or Blu-rays sharpened my grasp of films, even if they allowed me to check for mistakes in my descriptive writing. Like so much else in our cultural history, they disabled us more than they made us smarter or more observant, making us the servants of our machines rather than vice versa. I hope you won't think I'm off my rocker if I claim that our habit to make machines supposedly do our thinking for us is what led to the re-election of Donald Trump, a president who believes in algorithms more than people and someone for whom television played a major parental role. And, of course, people wanting to turn themselves into machines were around as early as Andy Warhol. People preferring their machines as companions to other people have been equally prevalent.

So, contrary to the myth of industrial progress via technology, I think we need to talk about devolution more than evolution, which is one reason why recently selling off most of my DVDs and Blu-rays felt liberating in some ways.

Traveling

Do you travel in America?

Recently, yes, but generally, no. I travel when I'm invited somewhere. *In Dreams Begin Responsibilities* was recently launched in Los Angeles, so I was there for a few days. This month I went to Iowa City and I've been invited to go to Berkeley, both in connection with the book. So I do like to travel, and, of course, I like it even more if I don't have to worry about jet lag—which is the case when I travel in the U.S. One thing that's complicated about my life now is that I have more friends in Paris and London and New

York than I do in Chicago. Most of my friends in Chicago have either moved away or died. I tend to be very reclusive, actually. I don't always like having this reclusive life, but on the other hand, through the Internet, I'm in touch with people all over the world. So it's a paradox.

Religion

What is your relationship with religion? I have the impression—though I could be wrong—that you tend to offer alternative readings of the works of directors who are often regarded as "religious filmmakers." Ermanno Olmi and Dreyer come to mind, for instance. Is this because you believe that a religious context might offer a limited, and perhaps less appealing, interpretation of these filmmakers' work?

I've been nonreligious since the age of twelve or so. My insistence on treating Dreyer as a nonreligious filmmaker stems directly from Maurice Drouzy's biography and a conversation I once had with Ib Monty, a friend of Dreyer's. As for Bresson and Olmi, I guess my materialist preferences and instincts tend to conflict with some of the transcendental aspects of their films seen by other critics. When Orson Welles in *This is Orson Welles* called Buñuel a deeply religious filmmaker, I think he may have been right and I was possibly wrong in overlooking this aspect of his work. But the most common critical typecasting I've encountered is probably the one treating Dreyer as religious, based on dubious sources and getting repeated endlessly.

A friend of mine, Daniela Michel,[*] once told me about visiting Buñuel's house in Mexico City. She was taken there by her uncle, who was a film producer. She mentioned that all the walls in his house were completely bare—there was no sign of any Oscar statuette or Palme d'Or. The only thing on the wall was a cross.

That makes sense.

Troubled Times

I don't watch TV. I only watch the news on TV when I'm traveling abroad and staying in a hotel room, mostly out of curiosity and to see how the news reportage format has

---

[*] Daniela Michel is the founding director of Morelia International Film Festival in Mexico.

changed. On October 7, 2023, I was in a hotel in Pordenone and was shocked to see that the atrocities in Israel and, a bit later, in Gaza, were reported like a movie—a badly made one.

One thing I formulate in *Camera Movements That Confound Us* is my definition of youth: the time when we think we can still distinguish between the news and entertainment. If you look at what is generally called the news now, it's indistinguishable in the U.S. from entertainment. It's all done as a show, and as I've said before, part of the whole confusion about Donald Trump has to do with this. I mean, is he a showbiz figure, or is he a politician? Do the two things work against each other? Do they work together? It seems to me that there is a lot of confusion right now because, at least in the U.S., we don't have news anymore. That's what it feels like.

You have lived through the Vietnam War, the genocide in the Balkans, the First Gulf War, and many other conflicts. Have you ever felt, at any point in your life, that what you do as a critic is really not enough? And, in fact, maybe it's a way of avoiding dealing with the problem in a more direct manner?

Not exactly, because I think, first of all, it's very hard to gauge the effect of writing on what happens in the world. But I was involved in politics before I was a film critic. I did certain things in the civil rights movement and the anti-war movement during the war in Vietnam. I don't know if they made a difference or not, but the point is that they certainly made a difference for me. Part of the problem is that people, in general, are not that well informed about what they're acting on. The fact that it's even harder to know now what's going on than it was before is very discouraging. So, it's hard to answer that question, except that if I knew that there was something I could do that could alleviate or change how much people are suffering, I might do it. But of course, one is never given that choice, right? So it becomes useless for me to speculate.

I remember once you said something very striking to me, that the U.S. was "the only country in the world that hates the arts." What did you mean by that?

I do think that Americans tend to hate art, and the reasons for this are at least partially based on a misunderstanding, an association of the arts with class. When people talk about art cinema, they always talk about things like serving cappuccino or wine in the theater lobby. In other words, things that, in people's minds, are associated with having money. That's something that's often spelled out literally in Woody Allen's films. Just look at how little state money is spent for the arts. It's often cited that in America there's more state money given to support military marching bands than to all the other arts combined. This already tells you that any country with that as a policy wouldn't be too friendly towards art and artists. What's so messed up about America is that a nonstop, neurotic and greedy compulsion to make money for its own sake is not even seen as questionable. It's seen as a normal, healthy attitude. Whereas art is seen as both pretentious and an unhealthy activity.

People associate art with men behaving like women or in a feminine manner. It's the sort of thing I got penalized for by bullies when I was a kid. And usually this has something to do with confusing art with money. This attitude goes back a long way. You can find it spelled out and analysed at great length by Alexis de Tocqueville.

In today's *New York Times*, on the front page, is a story about how they're afraid that Francis Coppola's new movie is going to lose money. In other words, this is seen as a disaster for everyone, society as a whole, which is preposterous. Then if you go to the arts section, there's a review of the film, but what's considered really important and newsworthy is the fact that some millionaires or billionaires whom we don't even know might lose money on this release. So many people judge things now in cinema as if they were the producers themselves. But why should we care about such a manufactured interest? It wasn't a concern when I was growing up; they didn't cite box office figures then the way they do now. This was something created by magazines like *Premiere*, reporting honestly, or sometimes dishonestly, how much films were making and how much the opening weekend grosses were. It wasn't a mainstream concern when I first got interested in film. It was a manufactured desire that was artificially created by the industry.

Donald Trump

What do you think about Donald Trump's re-election?

I was in denial at first, because a lot of people, including Michael Moore and me, believed that Kamala Harris was going to win. So, of course, it's extremely upsetting. The immediate reaction is yes, Americans really are that stupid and that racist and misogynous. But then I thought, well no, maybe their hatred of the Democratic Party for being so dismissive of them, the Trump supporters, is stronger and more relevant than their racism or sexism or their overall tolerance for Trump's nasty lies. I mean, we can always blame Trump for whipping up their hatred; that's easy enough to do. But what have we been doing to create all this hatred that Trump has been exploiting? How can we assume that such resentment was created out of thin air? What have we been ignoring and overlooking? It's like Americans asking rhetorically, after 9/11, "Why do they hate us?" and not even wanting to hear the answer—a question that may be as dumb as anything we can blame Trump's supporters for, when maybe the question should have been, "Why haven't we been paying enough attention to what we've been doing to people who live outside our bubble?"

It's also pertinent that what's happening in the U.S. is happening elsewhere in the world, including Britain. What was your reaction?

I was not surprised. I was very distressed, but not shocked somehow, because, as you said, I have seen it happening around me in Europe and elsewhere. But I was wondering because you've been working as a critic through different periods—occasionally challenging times in which you lived and worked and which shaped what you wrote as a film critic. How did that inform your work?

I think it often informs my work in ways that I'm not aware of. The results of the election are one example of my not being aware. Perhaps it's a case of being aware somewhat, but not as much as I should be, so it's a little hard to talk about, except that I obviously need to know what's going on in the world relative to what I'm writing about. I try to incorporate that as part of my writing, though obviously you don't really know what's going on until you get some distance from the period you're living in. It's like the joke I make in my book on camera movements that I've just finished. People on TV keep using the word "historical," that we're all living in a historical period, that's how important we are. But what they really mean by historical is hysterical. That's actually what's happening. There's a lot of hysteria, typified by how compulsively we talk about things and even ourselves as being "historical." But I'd like to know what periods are *ahistorical* and don't belong to history. This is as much of a con game as Trump claiming that Haitians are stealing and eating our cats and dogs.

Is that also "historical" or is it merely hysterical? Must we think that we're more important than the people who lived in other periods? My God, that's giving us more credit than anyone ever deserves to have! It's a sign of desperation, not lucidity.

Literature by Another Means

How free is your mind when you write?

I feel in all my writing there's a certain way in which the unconscious knows more than the conscious mind. I love the line—I think it's from E.M. Forster—"How do I know what I think until I see what I've said?" For me, writing is not simply taking an idea and running with it; it's also writing in order to find out what I think.

In the same way, when I used to write fiction, I was fascinated by the fact that at a certain point, the characters started doing things that I wasn't expecting, so I had to just follow them. The same thing can happen with ideas when I write now. Suddenly, the argument will take an unforeseen turn. That's really what makes it interesting.

If I say—and it's a controversial statement in some ways—that I think film criticism can be an art form, then what I'm doing is artistic work. And it's a position I can arrive at only because I'm not in the mainstream.

Do you get writer's block?

It's happened in the past, but not in recent years, although I do feel blocked now in playing my electric piano, maybe because I've forgotten so many of the chords I used to know.

You are one of the very few "first-person" film critics that I can think of.

Writing *Moving Places* made me more of a first-person writer than I had been before. I realized from writing the book that if you use the first person, readers will know where your ideas are coming from. There's a political reason for doing it, even though some people might say it's only because I'm self-centred. Maybe both things are true. Plus the fact that I'd started out seeing myself as an artist and a novelist and not as a film critic.

Do you tend to read other reviews of a film before writing your own?

It depends. Sometimes I do, sometimes I don't.

Duke Ellington used to compose music in any situation—while traveling, eating in a restaurant. Can you write in any environment, or do you need quiet and solitude to work?

I can write anywhere, but for some writing I need peace and quiet. When I don't have that, I'm more apt to be writing slogans.

When you write, are you afraid of repeating yourself, saying something that you have already said twenty years ago?

No. I figure that most of my audience—I mean, people who know my work really well—may say, "I've heard him say this before." But for the most part, the new context changes everything. I discovered that in *In Dreams Begin Responsibilities*, where I reconfigured my pieces in such a way that there's an ongoing theme of the relationship between music and literature and film. Somehow that changed the resonance of many of the pieces. Maybe the repetitions are tiresome for some readers, but if they were tiresome for me, I'd change or delete them.

I just wrote a piece about Kiarostami for a Canadian academic journal put out by an Iranian group. I put together pieces I'd already written as a starting point and then devised a new piece out of it. For me, recycling something is okay if it also involves reconfiguring.

When you put these things together to create a new work, this sort of collage—has it happened that by writing new passages, you kind of contradict what you had previously said and completely reconfigure the piece because of that?

Yes, it definitely can happen. I remember when Paul Verhoeven's *Basic Instinct* came out, I was anti-Verhoeven, and I gave it zero stars. Then I later came to think that I actually liked it. There was a way in which what was negative became positive.

The longest single piece in my new book, on Chantal Akerman, was commissioned by Adrian Martin and Girish Shambu's online magazine, *Lola*. Basically I put together all these pieces that I wrote, most of them for the *Reader*.

I don't think I changed my opinions much in that case, but combining several pieces changed the focus and the arguments.

In Dreams Begins Responsibilities *revisits some of the experimentation found in* Moving Places. *In this case, it features the jam session-like pairing of short and long pieces on jazz and cinema, and sometimes jazz in cinema. I found the book to embody the spirit of jazz arrangement, where familiar tunes are given new tonalities, colors and dynamics through the pens of Benny Carter, Bob Brookmeyer or Gil Evans. How did you decide on the "arrangement" for that?*

For me, the most valuable experimentation is the kind that makes otherwise inexpressible or at least unexpressed content possible. I believe that this is what motivated the experiments in *Moving Places.*

In the case of *In Dreams Begin Responsibilities*, I didn't even regard them as experiments. I wanted to include pieces of mine relating to film, literature and jazz, both capsule reviews and articles, and to order them chronologically. Your observation that the results are like jazz arrangements intrigues me, but this wasn't anything that I anticipated or consciously wanted. It's merely the results of decisions I made about content, leading to a certain truce between chance and control that's also integral to jazz arrangements—even arrangements of materials that don't necessarily include improvisation, like André Hodeir's *Anna Livia Plurabelle*, the focus of the book's last piece.

One of the last sections of *Moving Places* is titled "Chance and His Functions," which deliberately plays with the title of a crucial chapter in Noël Burch's *Theory of Film Practice*, "Chance and its Functions," factoring in the first name of the hero of Tennessee Williams' *Sweet Bird of Youth*, Chance Wayne, played by Paul Newman in both the stage and film versions, because the play and the film both figure prominently in this section. "Chance" isn't the same thing as "improvisation," which is a combination of chance and control, but I wanted to exploit the similarity when I titled this section, thereby demonstrating the functions of chance within my improvisation as a writer. The functions of chance within a controlled structure is what makes my new book resemble certain jazz arrangements.

A famous saying by Pierre Rissient goes, "It's not enough to like this movie. You have to like it for the right reasons." What do you think about this? Are there "right reasons" for liking a film? And who is the god deciding which reasons are right and which ones are wrong? It strikes me as nonsensical.

Yes, it's nonsensical, but also very, very French. It combines didacticism with passion in a way that I can appreciate even when I recognize its absurdity. Yet it's no more ridiculous than saying, "This was a good—or bad—year for cinema," which is very, very Anglo-American, and depends on so many intellectual shortcuts and unexamined assumptions that I almost wish it could be outlawed. The superiority of Pierre's solipsism over the Anglo-American nonsense is that it doesn't depend abjectly and unconsciously on capitalism, the way that we so often do. It's intellectual bullying, not economic bullying.

And there are formulas for approaching films that can lead to totally missing the point, like politique des auteurs. It's frustratingly limited, and it seems people like to limit themselves.

This is an ongoing problem. One of the films I consider in *Camera Movements That Confound Us* is *I Am Cuba*, where there are some extended, virtuoso camera movements that are executed not by individual cinematographers but by relay teams in which one cameraman passes the camera along to another. So the film's expressiveness can't be linked to a single auteur or to a way of assuming that "eye" equals "I."

The auteur theory was really important at one time because until the *Cahiers* group came along, Hitchcock was not even considered an artist, much less a serious artist. You can even say that the most singular success of the French New Wave was Truffaut's book on Hitchcock, because it belatedly convinced everybody that Hitchcock was a serious artist, something that hardly anyone would dispute today.

By the way, do you remember the two 16mm prints I sold to a suburban science teacher here in Chicago last month? He is going to screen one of them—Peter Bull's 45-minute MA thesis film in which I play the lead role, essentially playing myself, called *The Two-Backed Beast, or The Critic Makes the Film*—at the small auditorium of a major Chicago arthouse and former picture palace, the Music Box, along with two comic experimental shorts by Michael Snow (*Breakfast*) and Owen Land (*On the Marriage Broker Joke...*) that I selected, with the proceeds of the ticket sales going to me. I'll also be doing a book signing of *In Dreams* at the same event. It was very generous of Joshua Kim to set this up.

That's great news! Let me ask you another question: What makes criticism an art form when its starting point is examining another completed piece of art?

I think it has to do with the fact that it's a form of writing. I've often said that I considered myself a writer long before I considered myself a film critic. My ambition was to become a literary writer. It has a lot to do with the idea that, when I'm writing pieces, I'm actually thinking of them in literary terms, even my short capsule reviews. And I experiment a lot with the forms of criticism. I've done things that are unconventional in terms of how the pieces are put together. In other words, it's not about following a rigid set of rules.

If critics focus on textual analysis and an almost mathematical study of a film, do you think they miss the artistic or creative side of film criticism?

It depends, because some people use math as part of their art—Lewis Carroll, for example. Each case is different. I wouldn't want to make a blanket pronouncement, as there are as many kinds of film criticism as there are forms of other arts. All kinds of analysis can be done well or badly; they can be artful or mechanical. A lot of it has to do with the taste of the practitioner.

Memory Loss

It seems to me that cinema has lost some of its power of memory, even though more devices are now available to remind us of the past. I see an increasing number of films that show no awareness of what they owe to the past, both in terms of subject and style. One recent example for me was Soundtrack to a Coup d'État, *which seems unaware of Raoul Peck's* Lamumba *documentary and numerous other works on colonialism and jazz. I also feel that this loss of memory—or ignorance, depending on how you want to frame it—extends to critics, who often fail to recognize that there is a precedent for the film. I remember when* Rewind & Play, *about Thelonious Monk in France, was shown, nobody mentioned that Michael Cuscuna's Jazz Icons series had already released that French public television footage on DVD. The footage itself was incredibly revealing and required no intervention to expose racism and the troubling white perspective on Monk. Do you also feel this gradual loss of memory in cinema, or am I being too cynical?*

Memory is such a personal thing. I recently saw *Soundtrack to a Coup d'État* for the second time with Mehrnaz. She remembered not only the news of Lamumba's death when she was ten years old but also the fact that she knew that he was murdered by Americans, whereas I was already a teenager at the time, and the news of his death barely registered at all with me. My ignorance about who killed him and why had to wait until I saw this documentary at age 81. I'm ashamed to admit this, but it's a classic example of how innocent Americans can be. It also demonstrates the absurdity and futility of arguing that any film can be "objectively" good or bad for everyone in the world, as if we were all robots produced in the same assembly line. As it happens, both Mehrnaz and I have issues with how this film purports to document history even while we can appreciate certain aspects of it, but we can't escape the fact that it was made for dumb Americans like me and dumb Belgians like Johan Grimonprez, not for the smarter Iranians who already understood what was happening.

Cult Writer

What do you think about the so-called cult culture?

One of the reasons *Midnight Movies* is still in print is the public's ongoing fascination with cult movies. One argument I make in *In Dreams Begin Responsibilities* is recognizing that I have become, whatever my ambitions were, a cult writer. I now embrace this rather than reject it. I also use the term "niche market," because even though you get fewer people reading you in a niche market, the engagement is far more intense and meaningful, which is why this new collection is dedicated to the people who follow me on my website, my core audience. Most of that core is quite young, which is also interesting. According to Google Analytics, the people who read me the most are my youngest readers. And those who read me the least are members of my own generation. This could be because I'm probably more optimistic about film culture than most of my colleagues.

The point is, I would rather have a thousand readers who engage with me very passionately than a million readers who read me because I'm writing for *Time* magazine or *Newsweek* or *The New York Times*. In other words, if you're a cult writer or a niche market writer, then you can brand yourself. But if you're mainstream, it's the mainstream that brands you. I wrote my piece on Ingmar Bergman just after he died, at the behest of *The New York*

Times, and to a certain extent, what people were reacting to was the *Times*, rather than me.

Was the title of the article, "Scenes from an Overrated Career," the Times' *or yours?*

It was the *Times*' title, and I hated it because it was both cutesy in a flashy way and inaccurate, because there were no "scenes" in my article.

I'm not sure if your appeal is only based on your optimism. It's about a sense of excitement in the arguments you put forward. In fact, your readers can be quite pessimistic, but the core argument is always exciting. I think they respond to that, rather than to optimism.

I appreciate what you're saying. And I guess I can see that this would be part of it, too.

I'm not finished with optimism yet! There's a kind of optimism and being overtly positive that I find totally false. If you read The Guardian *reviews of new films, many of them get four or five stars. Then I go to the cinema to watch the films, and they are nowhere near that great. Sometimes, they're not even good films. So maybe there is some optimism in supporting arthouse cinema, even though the films don't deserve that kind of support.*

This reflects the fact that because regular film critics have to cover so many releases, including films they'd never choose to see on their own, they wind up being pathetically grateful for those that are only half decent, or maybe even one-third decent. Another side of this is the degree to which criticism as it exists is perceived by the industry as just one part of their publicity. Because they control access to the films, there's a certain way in which the reviews become part of their advertising. A review is coverage and coverage is promotion. So hype is encouraged.

More generally, I think that the expansion of hype and advertising into every corner of our lives is a central factor in our cultural decline, not just the decline of Hollywood. Even apart from the nightmare of having hundreds of ads every day in my spam folders, I often feel like I'm being smothered and suffocated to death by all the other ads that are blowing straight into my face whenever I try to breathe.

By now it has poisoned the public sector so completely that sometimes I feel that my reclusiveness is merely a form of self-preservation. When most of the language we encounter in our daily lives is both deceptive and inflated as a matter of routine, the triumph of a walking advertisement with built-in exclamation points like Donald Trump begins to seem inevitable. Voting him back into office is another way of saying, "Let the machines take care of us." When the sole purpose of the world communicating to us is to extract money from us, we have good reasons to stop paying attention, which is precisely what Trump wants.

Do you ever have the fantasy of making films?

Sure. As a child, I did this a lot, even specifically wanting to make a film about the Frank Lloyd Wright house. By the way, there was a period when Pierre Cottrell and Wim Wenders were working on *The American Friend* and they briefly considered using the Stanley Rosenbaum house as a location. This was because Nick Ray, who'd been a student of Wright's, was in the cast, But they quickly decided that flying everyone to Alabama would be too complicated and too expensive.

Anyway, what I liked about being a writer was that I didn't have to depend on anyone else's money and all I needed was a pen or pencil and some paper. What was always a turnoff for me about being a filmmaker was being totally dependent on other people and other people's money. I always thought the only way I could get involved in a film was to work with a director I admired, and this finally happened on *A House is Not a Home*. It didn't happen in Paris when Pierre Cottrell's wife Edith hired me to write *The Crystal World* because that wasn't something I would have chosen to have done myself.

Who are some of the contemporary filmmakers who have emerged since your retirement from the Reader *whose work excites you?*

Most recently, Radu Jude, Phạm Thiên Ân, and Patrick Wang. I've also been very impressed by Kaori Oda (a former student of mine at film.factory), and some if not all of the films of Kelly Reichardt and Alex Garland. I'm sure there are others, but these half-dozen are the first names that spring to mind.

Do you have any regrets?

Plenty. Above all, I regret my periodic loneliness and my lack of awareness of traits in myself that contributed to it. My father used to call me an "injustice collector" when I was a child, and I hope my various complaints in this book haven't given readers a similar impression.

Jonathan, I am going to arrange this book's chapters around countries and cities you have lived in. To me this is about the life of a sort of explorer who has worked in different cultural and social milieus. That drifting and exploring have also found their way into his writings. In the South, you were not a typical Southerner, mostly because your family was not a typical Southern family. In Paris, you were not a typically Parisian critic. In London, you were not a typical British reviewer. In New York, you resisted the traits of a classic New Yorker. In California, you found yourself unhappy and out of place. Eventually you found your place in Chicago because that city had no rigid preconditions or fixed expectations for how a critic should work.

Maybe that's true. By the way, I recently parted with my DVDs and Blu-rays. A Chicago pediatrician and hardcore cinephile named Dan Weissbluth who bought my video archive came and took them away this past Saturday. We're discussing the possibility of starting a film club next year in which I pick favorite items from my former collection to show and discuss in his screening room.

I'm sorry about your loss, but I think that was a good decision because someone else, or a group of people, is going to enjoy it. Plus, you get the money you need.

Yes, absolutely. And now I have a lot more shelf space for my books and my CDs! You might even say that these have become my fortress, my protection against more ads blowing into my face. If movies are really just a form of escapist entertainment, politics are currently doing an even better job of it.

APPENDIX: JONATHAN ROSENBAUM'S FAVORITE JAZZ RECORDINGS

Listed in order of the date of recording.

The Lester Young-Buddy Rich Trio: *I Want To Be Happy*
Lester Young (ts), Nat "King" Cole (p), Buddy Rich (d). Los Angeles, late March or early April, 1946. From the album *The Complete Lester Young & Nat King Cole Recordings*.

Original Charlie Parker Quintet: *Embraceable You*
Miles Davis (tp), Charlie Parker (as), Duke Jordan (p), Tommy Potter (b), Max Roach (d). New York City, October 28, 1947. From the album *The Complete Dial Sessions*.

Lennie Tristano Sextette: *Crosscurrent*
Lee Konitz (as), Warne Marsh (ts), Lennie Tristano (p), Billy Bauer (g), Arnold Fishkin (b), Harold Granowsky (d). New York City, March 4, 1949. From the album *Intuition*.

Miles Davis Nonet: *Boplicity*
Miles Davis (tp), J.J. Johnson (tb), Sandy Siegelstein (frh), Bill Barber (tu), Lee Konitz (as), Gerry Mulligan (bars, arr), John Lewis (p), Nelson Boyd, (b) Kenny Clarke (d), John Carisi, Gil Evans (arr). New York City, April 22, 1949. From the album *Birth of the Cool*.

André Hodeir: *Jazz et Jazz*
Roger Guérin (tp), Martial Solal (p), Jean Barraqué (electronics), Emmanuel Soudieux (b), Richie Frost (d), André Hodeir (arr). Paris, 1952. From the album *Jazz et Jazz*.

Louis Armstrong & His All Stars: *Long Gone*
Louis Armstrong (tp, voc), Trummy Young (tb), Barney Bigard (cl), Billy Kyle (p), Arvell Shaw (b), Barrett Deems (d), Velma Middleton (voc). Chicago, July 13, 1954. From the album *Louis Armstrong Plays W. C. Handy*.

Dave Brubeck: *In Your Own Sweet Way*
Dave Brubeck (p, solo). Oakland (Brubeck's house), April 18, 1956. From the album *Brubeck Plays Brubeck*.

Coleman Hawkins All Stars: *Bird Of Prey Blues*
Buck Clayton (tp), Coleman Hawkins (ts), Hank Jones (p), Ray Brown (b), Mickey Sheen (d). New York City, February 18 or 19, 1958. From the album *The High and Mighty Hawk*.

Ahmad Jamal: *Darn That Dream*
Ahmad Jamal (p), Israel Crosby (b), Vernell Fournier (d). San Francisco, late 1961. From the album *At the Blackhawk*.

Charles Mingus Sextet: *Peggy's Blue Skylight*
Eric Dolphy (as, bcl, fl), Clifford Jordan (ts), Jaki Byard (p), Charles Mingus (b), Dannie Richmond (d). Salle Wagram, Paris, France, April 17, 1964. From the album *Charles Mingus in Paris: The Complete America Session*.

John Coltrane Quartet: *Wise One*
John Coltrane (ts), McCoy Tyner (p), Jimmy Garrison (b), Elvin Jones (d). Englewood Cliffs, New Jersey, April 27, 1964. From the album *Crescent*.

Wynton Marsalis Quartet: *Juan*
Wynton Marsalis (tp), Marcus Roberts (p), Robert Leslie Hurst III (b), Jeff "Train" Watts (d). Washington D. C., December 19 or 20, 1986. From the album *Live at Blues Alley*.

Keith Jarrett: *Bop-Be*
Keith Jarrett (p), Gary Peacock (b), Jack DeJohnette (d). New York City, June 3 or 4, 1994. From the album *At the Blue Note*.

BIBLIOGRAPHY

Rivette: Texts and Interviews (edited and introduced), British Film Institute, 1977

Moving Places: A Life at the Movies, Harper & Row and Harper Colophon, 1980; second edition, University of California Press, 1995

Film: The Front Line 1983, Arden Press, 1983

Midnight Movies (with J. Hoberman), Harper & Row, 1983; second edition, Da Capo Press, 1991

This Is Orson Welles (by Orson Welles and Peter Bogdanovich; edited and annotated), Harper Collins, 1992; second edition, Da Capo Press, 1998; also produced and edited four-hour audiocassette version for Harper Audio/Caedmon, 1992

Greed, British Film Institute, 1993

Placing Movies: The Practice of Film Criticism, University of California Press, 1995

Movies as Politics, University of California Press, 1997

Joe Dante et les Gremlins de Hollywood (co-edited with Bill Krohn), Cahiers du Cinéma/Locarno International Film Festival, 1999

Dead Man, British Film Institute, 2000; second edition, 2001

Movie Wars: How Hollywood and the Media Limit What Films We Can See, A Cappella Books, 2000

Movie Mutations: The Changing Face of World Cinephilia (co-edited with Adrian Martin), British Film Institute, 2003

Abbas Kiarostami (with Mehrnaz Saeed-Vafa), University of Illinois Press, 2003; expanded Argentinian edition, 2014; expanded U.S. edition, 2018

Essential Cinema: On the Necessity of Film Canons, Johns Hopkins University Press, 2004; expanded paperback edition, 2008

Discovering Orson Welles, University of California Press, 2007

The Unquiet American: Transgressive Comedies from the U.S., Viennale/Austrian Filmmuseum, 2009

Goodbye Cinema, Hello Cinephilia, University of Chicago Press, 2010

Cinematic Encounters: Interviews and Dialogues, University of Illinois Press, 2018

Cinematic Encounters 2: Portraits and Polemics, University of Illinois Press, 2019

In Dreams Begin Responsibilities: A Jonathan Rosenbaum Reader, Hat & Beard Press, 2024

Travels in the Cities of Cinema (with Ehsan Khoshbakht), Sticking Place Books, 2025

Camera Movements That Confound Us, Sticking Place Books (forthcoming)

INDEX

Corpus Collosum (Snow), 79

2/*Duo* (Suwa), 145
2 or 3 Things I Know About Her (Godard), 86
24 Frames (Kiarostami), 114
2001: A Space Odyssey (Kubrick), 28

ABC Africa (Kiarostami), 112
Accident (Losey), 66
Adair, Gilbert, 61, 67, 80
Adderley, Cannonball, 23
Advise and Consent (Preminger), 38
Aelita (Protazanov), 50
Aerograd (Dovzhenko), 59
African Queen, The (Huston), 117
Agee, James, 29
Akerman, Chantal, 50, 54, 76, 153
Alexander Nevsky (Eisenstein), 20
Algiers (Cromwell), 125
Allen, Woody, 117, 150
Almanac of Fall (Tarr), 141
Alspecter, Lisa, 133
Altman, Robert, 41, 85
American Cinema: Directors and Directions 1929-1968 (Sarris), 37, 86
American Film, 124
American Friend, The (Wenders), 72
Amour fou, L' (Rivette), 41, 76
Andersen, Thom, 99
Andrews, Nigel, 55
Angel Face (Preminger), 76
An Illustrated History of the Horror Film (Clarens), 39
Anna Livia Plurabelle (Hodeir), 44, 154
Annie Get Your Gun (Sidney/Berkeley), 14

Antonioni, Michelangelo, 22, 129
Apocalypse Now (Coppola), 96, 140
Apostle, The (Duvall), 125
Arendt, Hannah, 20-21
Armstrong, Louis, 23
At the Movies, 99
Avventura, L' (Antonioni), 28

Baby Doll (Kazan), 19
Baker, Chet, 26
Bals, Huub, 93, 123
Ballard, J.G., 41
Bani-Etemad, Rakhshan, 122
Bard Observer, 21
Barthes, Roland, 65
Bartók, Béla, 11
Basic Instinct (Verhoeven), 153
Bazin, André, 56, 80
Beatty, Warren, 102
Begone Dull Care (McLaren), 20
Bellour, Raymond, 64, 108-109
Belmondo, Jean-Paul, 25
Benamou, Catherine, 127
Benayoun, Robert, 117
Bergman, Ingmar, 145, 157
Best Years of Our Lives, The (Wyler), 114
Bigger Than Life (Ray), 52
Big Red One, The (Fuller), 88
Bird of Paradise (Daves), 14
Birth of a Nation, The (Griffith), 31
Biskind, Peter, 102
Bitter Victor (Ray), 33
Black and Tan (Murphy), 60
Bloom, Harold, 110
Blücher, Heinrich, 20-21
Bogdanovich, Peter, 59, 124
Bonjour Mr. Lewis (Benayoun), 117
Borges, Jorge Luis, 44

Boudu Saved from Drowning
 (Renoir), 100, 103
Boy (Lewis), 116
Bragin, John, 30
Brakhage, Stan, 31, 77
Breakfast (Snow), 155
Breathless (Godard), 20, 28, 115
Brecht, Bertolt, 82
Brenez, Nicole, 118-19
Bresson, Robert, 20, 38, 49, 112, 148
Brewster, Ben, 63
Brick and Mirror (Golestan), 105
Brookmeyer, Bob, 154
Brubeck, Dave, 23
Bruegel, Pieter, 21
Bull, Peter, 24, 155
Buñuel, Luis, 103, 148
Burch, Noël, 36-37, 154
Burnett, Charles, 100
Bush, George W., 97, 133

Cahiers du Cinéma, 29-30, 38,
 42-43, 50-52, 59, 109, 155
Caimán Cuadernos de Cine, 118
Callenbach, Ernest, 82
*Camera Movements That
 Confound Us* (Rosenbaum),
 2, 132, 149, 155
Camera Obscura, 74
Cameron, Ian, 64
Carroll, Lewis, 156
Carroll, Noël, 77
Carter, Benny, 154
Carter, Ron, 24
Cassavetes, John, 104
Cat People (Tourneur), 76
Céline and Julie Go Boating
 (Rivette), 40, 49, 60-61, 76
Chambers, Paul, 23
Chaplin, Charlie, 101-102, 117
Chaplin, Geraldine, 41
Chase, Chevy, 24
Chekhov, Anton, 81
Chicago Reader, vii, 2, 5, 52, 54-55,
 60, 77, 79, 87, 92-99, 103-104,
 106, 110, 120, 130-35, 137,
 141, 146, 153
Chicago Tribune, 100
Christmas in July (Sturges), 26
Chytilová, Věra, 22
Ciment, Michel, 43-44
Cineaste, 43, 99
Cinema: A Critical Dictionary
 (Roud), 86
Cinema Book, The (Cook), 63
Cinema of Carl Dreyer, The
 (Milne), 56
Cinema Papers, 118

*Cinematic Encounters: Interviews
 and Dialogues* (Rosenbaum),
 118
Cioran, E.M., 115
Citizen Kane (Welles), 20, 32, 53,
 63, 127
City Lights (Chaplin), 20
Clarens, Carlos, 39
Clark, Larry, 71
*Close Encounters of the Third
 Kind* (Spielberg), 72
Close-Up (Kiarostami), 113
Cocteau, Jean, 80
Coffee and Cigarettes (Jarmusch),
 110
Coleman, John, 62
Coleman, Ornette, 23
Coltrane, John, 23
Combs, Richard, 47-49
Compound Cinema, The
 (Potamkin), 29
Confidence (Szabó), 85
Connection, The (Clark), 76
Connection, The (Gelber), 20
Contemporary Cinema, The
 (Houston), 46
Cook, Pam, 63
Coppola, Francis, 5, 140, 146, 150
Corbyn, Jeremy, 12
Corliss, Richard, 85
Corman, Roger, 113
Costa, Pedro, 107
Cottrell, Edith, 38, 41, 159
Cottrell, Pierre, 38, 159
Coutard, Raoul, 115
Cozarinsky, Edgardo, 108
Cronin, Paul, 43
Crosby, Bing, 102
Crown Jewels of Iran, The
 (Golestan), 106
Crowther, Bosley, 29, 101, 103
Crying Game, The (Jordan), 99
Crystal World, The (Ballard), 41, 159
Cuadecuc, vampir (Portabella),
 77, 107
Curtis, Adam, ix
Curtis, Tony, 117
Curtiss, Thomas Quinn, 96
Cuscuna, Michael, 156

Daisy Miller (Bogdanovich), 49
Damnation (Tarr), 141
Damned, The (Losey), 66
Damn Yankees, 116
Daney, Serge, 42, 94, 107, 117
Danner, Blythe, 24
Dante, Joe, 113
Dargis, Manohla, 94

Dark Passage (Daves), 76
David Holtzman's Diary (McBride), 43
Davis, Miles, 23
Dead, The (Huston), 129
Dead Don't Die, The (Jarmusch), 110
Dead Man (Jarmusch), 84, 103, 109-110
de Baecque, Antoine, 109
Deep Cover (Duke), 103
Deer Hunter, The (Cimino), 96, 119
de Gregorio, Eduardo, 40, 49, 61, 67, 107
Deems, Barrett, 23
Demoiselles de Rochefort, Les (Demy), 55
de Oliveira, Manoel, 112
De Palma, Brian, 42
De Sica, Vittorio, 114
de Tocqueville, Alexis, 150
De Toth, Andre, x
Deux Fois (Raynal), 75
Discovering Orson Welles (Rosenbaum), 124
Disney, Walt, 10
Dog Star Man (Brakhage), 32
Don Quixote (Cervantes), 110
Don Quixote (Welles), 127
Doomed Love (de Oliveira), 112
Dorham, Kenny, 23
Dovzhenko, Alexander, 50, 59-60
Dreyer, Carl, 29, 56, 102, 140, 148
Dreyfus, Liliane, 37
Driver, Sarah, 110, 123
Drouzy, Maurice, 148
Dr. Mabuse (Lang), 59
Dr. Strangelove (Kubrick), 21, 30
Dubliners (Joyce), 94
Duchin, Eddy, 10
Duelle (Rivette), 58, 61, 76
Duke, Bill, 103
Duke Ellington and His World (Lawrence), 60
Duras, Marguerite, 76
Durgnat, Raymond, ix, 29, 56-57, 71, 74, 82, 111
Dutt, Guru, 38
Duvall, Robert, 125

Ebert, Roger 99-100, 103, 114
Eckert, Charles, 81
Eclipse (Antonioni), 28
Eddy Duchin Story, The (Sidney), 10
Edge, The (Kramer), 76
Eisenschitz, Bernard, 37-38, 64
Eisenstein, Sergei, 50, 82, 84

Eisner, Lotte, 36, 41
Ellington, Duke, 60, 153
Elmer Gantry (Brooks), 92
Enchanted Desna, The (Solntseva), 50
English, Deidre, 96
Endfield, Cy, 65
Engels, Friedrich, 62
Eraserhead (Lynch), 83
Essential Cinema (Rosenbaum), 104
Esquire, 28
Evans, Bill, 23, 44
Evans, Gil, 154

Face in the Crowd, A (Kazan), 19
Family Plot (Hitchcock), 49
Farber, Manny, x, 25-26, 29, 48, 54, 57, 70, 72, 108, 111
Fassbinder, Rainer Werner, 129
Fatal Attraction (Lynne), 96
Fei, Mu, 26
Femmes au soleil (Dreyfus), 37
Ferguson, Otis, 29
Ferreri, Marco, 39
F for Fake (Welles), 4, 40-41, 73, 128
Film Comment, 39, 42, 54, 64, 71, 76, 79-80, 82, 85, 124, 142
Film Culture, 29
film.factory, 77, 141-44, 159
Films and Feeling (Durgnat), 29
Film Masters (Rosenbaum), 30
Film Quarterly, 82, 105, 124, 126
Film: The Front Line 1983 (Rosenbaum), 77-79, 110
Financial Times, 55, 60
Finler, Joel, 46
Fitzgerald, F. Scott, 36
Flaming Creatures (Smith), 78
Flitterman-Lewis, Sandy, 74-75, 82, 85, 92
Florence Times, The, 80
Foolish Wives (von Stroheim), 86
Forbes, Jill, 80
Foreman, Richard, 85
For Ever Mozart (Godard), 107
Forster, E.M., 152
Four Nights of a Dreamer (Bresson), 38-39
Fradelič, Sunčica, 143
Framework, 82
Frampton, Hollis, 107
Franco, Francisco, 67, 107, 121
Freaks (Browning), 15
Fritts, Donnie, 23
Fujiwara, Chris, 119
Fuller, Samuel, 32, 71, 88-89, 99, 117
Full Metal Jacket (Kubrick), 95

Gabel, J.C., 55
Garland, Alex, 159
Geffen, Sid, 75
Geng, Veronica, 76, 82, 85
Gentlemen Prefer Blondes (Hawks), 59, 76
Gertrud (Dreyer), 56, 141
Ghost Dog (Jarmusch), 110
Gianvito, John, 99
Gidal, Peter, 65
Glass Menagerie, The (Williams), 12
Glen and Randa (McBride), 43
Go-Between, The (Losey), 66
Godard, Jean-Luc, xi, 5, 22, 25, 28, 33, 56, 57, 64, 71, 79, 86, 87-88 88, 99, 107, 109, 114-115, 119
Godard on Godard (Milne), 46
Godfather Part II, The (Coppola), 49
Golestan, Ebrahim, 105-106
Gorfinkel, Elena, 104
Gorin, Jean-Pierre, 25, 71
Gough-Yates, Kevin, 61
Graham, Michael, 61
Graham, Pat, 98
Grand Bouffe, La (Ferreri)
Grand Illusion, The (Renoir), 28
Graver, Gary, 71
Great Consoler, The (Kuleshov), 58
Great Garrick, The (Whale), 49
Greed (von Stroheim), 46, 108, 111
Green, Aaron, 15
Greenspun, Roger, 77, 94
Greenbaum, Connie, 38-39
Griffith, D.W., 114
Grimonprez, Johan, 157
Gronvall, Andrea, 99
Guardian, The, 158

Hamilton, Chico, 23
Hampton, Lionel, 26
Hamrah, A.S., 130
Hancock, Herbie, 24
Handy, W.C., 15, 19
Hardly Working (Lewis), 116
Harris, Kamala, 150
Hartley, L.P., 66
Harvey, Stephen, 82
Hasumi, Shiguehiko, 33, 100
Hawks, Howard, 32
Heart of Darkness (Welles), 40
Heath, Stephen, 50, 62, 84
Hedren, Tippi, 113
Hegel, Georg, 21
Heidegger, Martin, 20-21
Hemingway, Ernest, 36
Herrmann, Bernard, 63
Heston, Charlton, 125-26, 128

Hillier, Jim, 50
Hiroshima mon amour (Resnais), 20, 28
Histoire(s) du Cinéma (Godard), 107
Hitchcock, Alfred, 32, 101-102, 155
Hitchcock's Films (Wood), 50
Hoberman, Jim, 83, 113, 142
Hock, Louis, 71, 74, 111
Hodeir, André, 44, 154
Hollywood Story, The (Finler), 46
Hoover, J. Edgar, 19
Hope, Bob, 102
Hopper, Dennis, 128
Hopper/Welles (Welles), 128
Horla, Le (Pollet), 76
Hotel New York (Raynal), 76
House is Not a Home: Wright or Wrong, A (Saeed-Vafa), 12-13, 24, 115-16, 159
House of Bamboo (Fuller), 76
House of Wax (De Toth), 15
Houston, Penelope, 29, 46-48, 51-53, 56, 59, 61-63, 70, 132
Howard, Noah, 24
Hubbard, L. Ron, 30
Huckleberry Finn (Twain), 12
Huillet, Danièle, 49
Huston, John, 127, 129-30

I Am Cuba (Kalatozov), 155
Indian Tomb, The (Lang), 38
In Dreams Begin Responsibilities (Rosenbaum), ix, 3-5, 21, 55, 136-37, 147, 153-55, 157
International Herald Tribune, 96
In the Realm of the Senses (Ōshima), 63
Intolerance (Griffith), 8
Ishtar (May), 102
I Walked with a Zombie (Tourneur), 76

Jackson, Laura Riding, 107
Jacobs, Ken, 58, 78
Jamal, Ahmad, 23, 25
James, Henry, 66
Jameson, Richard, 124
Jancsó, Miklós, 22
Jarmusch, Jim, 84, 99, 106, 109, 123
Jarrett, Keith, 26
Jazz in the Movies (Meeker), 50
Jazz on a Summer's Day (Stern), 145
Jeanne Dielman, 23 quai du Commerce, 1080 Bruxelles (Akerman), 49-50, 53, 70
Jerry and Me (Saeed-Vafa), 116
Johnson, J.J., 23
Jones, Kent, 113, 118

Jones, Philly Joe, 23
Jost, Jon, 71, 100
Joyce, James, 36, 44
Jude, Radu, 122, 159
Junior Scholastic, 10

Kabir, Nasreen Munni, 38-39
Kael, Pauline, 63, 86-87
Karina, Anna, 86
Karlson, Phil, 19
Kauffmann, Stanley, 29
Kazan, Elia, 19-20
Keaton, Buster, 59
Kehr, Dave, 53, 87, 92-95, 98, 100, 131, 134
Kelly, Grace, 10
Kelly, Robert, 31
Kenton, Stan, 23
Khrushchev, Nikita, 22
Kiarostami, Abbas, vii, 112-115, 121, 153
Killing Fields, The (Joffé), 103
Kim, Joshua, 155
King, Martin Luther, 19
King Kong (Cooper/Schoedsack), 81
King Lear (Godard), 107
Kinoshita, Keiko 33
Kirk, Roland, 23
Klein, William, 141
Koch, Stephen, 36
Kodar, Oja, 124, 127-29, 144
Konitz, Lee, 23
Koza, Roger, 104
Kristofferson, Kris, 23
Krohn, Bill, 113
Kubrick, Stanley, 43, 52
Kuleshov, Lev, 58

Lady in the Lake (Montgomery), 76
LaFaro, Scott, 23
Lancelot du Lac (Bresson), 49
Lambert, Gavin, 51-52
Land, Owen, 155
Lane, Anthony, 107
Lang, Fritz, 38, 59
Langlois, Henri, 39
Lanzmann, Claude, 37
Last Laugh, The (Murnau), 31
Last Night of Les Halles, The (Siegler), 42
Last Year at Marienbad (Resnais), 28, 52, 77, 115
Lawrence, A.H., 61
Léaud, Jean-Pierre, 41, 77
Lee, Kevin, 99, 141
Legrand, Michel, 128
Leigh, Janet, 117, 125-26
Lelouch, Claude, 40

Lelyveld, Joseph, 11, 94
Lenehan, Michael, 92
Let's Get Lost (Weber), 26
Lewis, Jerry, 32, 55, 116-117, 119
Lewis, Joel, 75
Libération, 109
Life and Nothing More (Kiarostami), 113
Light in August (Faulkner), 94
Lion Hunters, The (Rouch), 76
Little Night Music, A (Sondheim), 67
Living Theatre, The, 20
Loeb, Sylvia, 48
Lola, 153
London Review of Books, 96
Lopate, Phillip, 52
Lopez, Jennifer, 108
Los Angeles Times, The, 82
Losey, Joseph, 43, 65-67, 129
Luddy, Tom, 71, 107
Lumumba (Peck), 156

MacCabe, Colin, 62, 64
Macdonald, Dwight, 28
Macdonald, Nick, 28, 136
Maddin, Guy, 107
Made in USA (Godard), 88
Magic Flute, The (Bergman), 145
Magazine of Fantasy and Science Fiction, The, 10
Maîtres fous, Les (Rouch), 76
Makavejev, Dušan, 22
Malcolm, Derek, 67
Malick, Terrence, 108
Malle, Justine, 84
Malle, Louis, 84
Manchurian Candidate, The (Demme), 133
Manchurian Candidate, The (Frankenheimer), 133
Mancini, Henry, 125
Mans, Lorenzo, 43
Man Who Would Be King, The (Huston), 129
Markopoulos, Gregory, 77
Marks, Scott, 116
Marsh, Wayne, 22
Martian Chronicles, The (Bradbury), 12
Martin, Adrian, 113, 118, 153
Martin, Dean, 117
Marx, Karl, 21
Maslin, Janet, 109, 132
Masumura, Yasuzo, 33
May, Elaine, 102
Mayersberg, Paul, 64
McArthur, Colin, 62
McBride, Jim, 43, 71

McCarthy, Joseph, 66, 127-28
McCarthy, Todd, 82
McKay, Ralph 122
McLaren, Norman, 20
McNaught, Rowan, 135
Mediterranée (Pollet), 76
Meeker, David, 50-51
Megalopolis (Coppola), 5, 140, 146
Mehrjui, Dariush, 121
Mekas, Jonas, 77-78, 115
Mélo (Resnais), 95
Mépris, Le (Godard), 76
Merchant of Venice, The (Shakespeare), 11
Merman, Cynthia, 80-82
Merry-Go-Round (Rivette), 76
Midnight Movies (Rosenbaum/Hoberman), 83, 113, 124, 157
Michel, Daniela, 148
Michelson, Annette, 79
Milne, Tom, 29, 46, 50, 55-56, 82
Mingus, Charlie, 23, 25
Miracle, The (Rossellini), 76
Mirror for England, A (Durgnat), ix
Mise en Scène and Film Style (Martin), 118
Mississippi Burning (Parker), 19, 103
Mizoguchi, Kenji, 33
Modern Jazz Quartet, 23
Mongols, The (Kimiavi), 51
Monk, Thelonious, 23, 25, 156
Monroe, Marilyn, 66
Monsieur Verdoux (Chaplin), 103
Monthly Film Bulletin, 47, 49, 53, 56, 60-61, 63, 131
Monty, Ib, 148
Moonfleet (Lang), 76
Moore, Michael, 150
Morgenstern, Don, 24
Morrissey, Paul, 37
Moses and Aaron (Straub/Huillet), 49
Mother and the Whore, The (Eustache), 38
Moullet, Luc, 70
Movie, 64
Moviegoer, 29
Movie Man (Thomson), 29
Movie Mutations (Rosenbaum/Martin), 113, 118
Movie Wars (Rosenbaum), 136
Moving Places (Rosenbaum), 9, 13-14, 58, 70-71, 74-75, 79, 81-82, 86, 89, 108, 111, 116, 118, 124, 146-47, 152, 154
Mr. Freedom (Klein), 141
Müller, Marco, 113
Mulvey, Laura, 58, 64

Murch, Walter, 124-26
Muriel (Resnais), 28
Murawski, Bob, 128
Murnau, F.W., 119
Musk, Elon, 130
Myles, Lynda, 58
Mystery Train (Jarmusch), 110

Naked Lunch (Burroughs), 82
Naremore, James, 53, 105, 111, 113, 146
Nashville (Altman), 41, 49
Nelson, Craig, 83, 124
New Masses, The, 29
Newman, Paul, 154
New Statesman, 62
Newsweek, 157
New Yorker, The, 85, 97, 107, 109
New York Film Bulletin, 29
New York Herald Tribune, 121
New York Review of Books, 130
New York Stories (Raynal), 76
New York Times, The, 11, 29, 86, 93-94, 101, 109, 132, 150, 157-58
New York Times Book Review, The, 83
Neve, Brian, 66
Nichols, Mike, 102
Nietzsche, Friedrich, 21
Night of the Hunter, The (Grubb), 12
Night on Earth (Jarmusch), 110
No Country for Old Men (Coen), 96
Notes of a Native Son (Baldwin), 94
Not Reconciled (Straub), 76
Noroît (Rivette), 41, 61, 76-77
Nouvelle Vogue (Godard), 87

Obama, Barack, 102
Occasional Work of a Female Slave (Kluge), 46
Oda, Kaori, 159
Ogier, Bulle, 41
Olmi, Ermanno, 148
Only Lovers Left Alive (Jarmusch), 110
On Moonlight Bay (Del Ruth), 81, 89
On the Marriage Broker Joke... (Land), 155
On the Waterfront (Kazan), 75, 117
On Totalitarianism (Arendt), 20
Orphée (Cocteau), 76
Ōshima, Nagisa, 63
Other Side of the Wind, The (Welles), 127-29
Oui, 37

Out 1 (Rivette), 41, 141
Out 1: Spectre (Rivette), 25, 49, 76
Outfoxed: Rupert Murdoch's War on Journalism (Greenwald), 97
Out of Sight (Soderbergh), 108
Overby, David, 93
Ozu, Yasujirō, 25, 43, 63, 100

Pakula, Alan, 42
Paris Belongs to Us (Rivette), 20, 76
Parker, Charlie, x
Party Girl (Ray), 76
Pasolini, Pier Paolo, 63, 65
Passer, Ivan, 99
Passing Through (Clark), 71
Paterson (Jarmusch), 110
Patterson, Patricia, 70, 73
Peck, Raoul, 156
Peña, Richard, 107
Perez, Gilberto, 119
Perkins, V.F., 64
Permanent Vacation (Jarmusch), 110
Peterson, Oscar, 23
Petit, Chris, 54
Phạm, Thiên Ân, 159
Phenix City Story, The (Karlson), 19
Picasso, Pablo, 114
Pickpocket (Bresson), 20
Pierrot le fou (Godard), 25
Pinter, Harold, 66, 129
Placing Movies (Rosenbaum), 43, 110-111, 116, 118
Plaisir du texte, Le (Barthe), 37
PlayTime (Tati), 24, 34, 42
Platoon (Stone), 95
Pollet, Jean-Daniel, 76
Portabella, Pere, 77-78
Positif, 43
Potamkin, Harry Alan, 29
Pourquoi Israël (Lanzmann), 37
Powell, Bud, 23
Praxis du Cinéma (Theory of Film Practice) (Burch), 37, 154
Premiere, 150
Preminger, Otto, 62
Presents (Snow), 79
Pretty Woman (Marshall), 95
Proust, Marcel, 47, 66
Psycho (Van Sant), 133
Pynchon, Thomas, 81

Radio Days (Allen), 95
Rameau's Nephew by Diderot (Snow), 49
Rappaport, Mark, 99, 107
Ray, Nicholas, 20, 34, 52, 88, 159
Ray, Satyajit, 114
Raynal, Jackie, 75-76

Rear Window (Hitchcock), 10
Redgrave, Vanessa, 62
Région centrale, La (Snow), 79
Reichardt, Kelly, 159
Religieuse, La (Rivette), 76
Renoir, Jean, 76, 82, 100
Resnais, Alain, 33, 39, 95
Rewind & Play (Gomis), 156
Reygadas, Carlos, 143
Riambau, Esteve, 127-28
Rimbaud, Arthur, 81
Rickey, Carrie, 75
Richie, Donald, 43
Rissient, Pierre, 154-55
Rivette, Jacques, 20, 39-41, 50-51, 52 53, 58, 61, 67, 76-77, 84, 107, 144
Rivette: Texts and Interviews (Rosenbaum), 76
Rocky Horror Picture Show, The (Sharman), 83
Rohmer, Eric, 38, 76
Romero, George, 83
Rosebud (Preminger), 62
Rossellini, Roberto, 51
Rouch, Jean, 99-100
Roud, Richard, 55
Round Midnight (Tavernier), 95
Ruins Within (Saeed-Vafa), 111-12
Rumble Fish (Coppola), 146

Saddest Music in the World, The (Maddin), 107
Saeed-Vafa, Mehrnaz, 12, 23-24, 51, 105, 111, 114-116, 121, 140-41, 157
Safran, Yehuda, 46
Sailor Beware (Walker), 117
Salò (Pasolini), 63, 65
Sarris, Andrew, 29-30, 36-37, 77, 86-87
Sátántangó (Tarr), 44, 142
Saving Private Ryan (Spielberg), 108
Sayles, John, 75
Scénario(s) (Godard), 57
Schmidlin, Rick, 60, 124-25
Schmidt, Paul, 81
Schwartz, Delmore, 81
Scorsese, Martin, 113
Scotch Reels (McArthur), 62
Scott, A.O., 94
Scott-Moncrieff, C.K., 47
Scott-Moncrieff, Sue, 47
Screen, 51, 56, 58, 62-65, 70, 76
Screen Education, 62
Seberg, Jean, 41
Sedofsky, Lauren, 67
Seed of the Sacred Fig, The (Rasoulof), 105

Sérail (de Gregorio), 107
Servant, The (Losey), 66
Sesonke, Alexander, 77, 92
Seton, Marie, 50
Seventh Victim, The (Robson), 76
Shadows (Cassavetes), 20, 28
Shakespeare, William 133
Shambu, Girish, 153
Shepp, Archie, 23
Shivas, Mark, 64
Shylock on the Stage (Lelyveld), 11
Siegler, Marie-France, 42
Sight and Sound, 5, 29, 39, 46-47, 49, 51-53, 56, 61-64, 70, 82 103, 105, 132
Silence of the Lambs, The (Demme), 96
Silent Majority (Saeed-Vafa), 112
Simmons, Jean, 67
Sinatra, Frank, 75
Singin' in the Rain (Kelly/Donen), 117
Siskel, Gene, 99-100
Sitney, P. Adams, 79
Smith, Jack, 78
Smith, Zadie, 130
Snow, Michael, 49, 79, 155
Soderbergh, Steven, 108
Soho News, 76, 82-85, 88, 99
Solal, Martial, 23
Solntseva, Yuliya, 50
Something Different (Chytilová), 76
Sontag, Susan, 21, 32, 41
Soundtrack to a Coup d'État (Grimonprez), 156-57
Speaking Directly (Jost), 49
Spielberg, Steven, 108
Spock, Benjamin, 11
Spring in a Small Town (Fei), 26
Stargazer (Koch), 36
Star Wars (Lucas), 96
Stavisky (Resnais), 39
Stein, Elliott, 81, 86
Steve Lacy: Lift the Bandstand (Bull), 24
Stoller, Jim, 29
Stop Smiling, 55
Story of Adele H., The (Truffaut), 80
Stranger, The (Welles), 126
Stranger Than Paradise (Jarmusch), 110
Straub, Jean-Marie, 49, 79
Stravinsky, Igor, 11
Structural Film Anthology (Gidal), 65
Sturges, Preston, 26, 52
Sunrise (Murnau), 31-32
Sun Shines Bright, The (Ford), 141

Suwa, Nobuhiro, 145
Sweet Bird of Youth (Williams), 154
Swinton, Tilda, 144

Tamura, Masaki, 145
Tanaka, Kinoya, 33
Tarr, Béla, 43, 77, 106-107, 122, 140-44
Tashlin, Frank, 32
Taste of Cherry, A (Kiarostami), 114
Tati, Jacques, 34, 39, 42, 55, 115, 145
Taubin, Amy, 84-85
Tavernier, Bertrand, x, 95
Taylor, Billy, 23
Tenant, The (Polanski), 49
Theory of Film Practice (Burch), see *Praxis du Cinéma*
Thin Red Line, The (Malick), 108
Thing from Another World, The (Nyby), 15
This Could Be the Night (Wise), 71
This is Orson Welles (Rosenbaum), 58, 83, 124, 148
Thomson, David, 29
Thornton, Leslie, 107
Tiger of Eschnapur, The (Lang), 38
Time, 132, 157
Time Out, 39, 54
Tobin, Dan, 127
Tom, Tom, the Piper's Son (Jacobs), 58
Toot, Whistle, Plunk and Boom (Kimball/Nichols), 10
Tourneur, Jacques, 119, 145
To Sleep With Anger (Burnett), 100
Touch of Evil (Welles), 49-50, 60, 117, 124-26, 128
Tout va bien (Godard/Gorin), 39
Trafic, 64, 107-108, 124, 126
True, Alison, 52, 132-34
Truffaut, François, 32-33, 80, 155
Trump, Donald, 4, 102, 130, 147, 149-51, 159
Turin Horse, The (Tarr), 142
Twin Peaks (Lynch), 97
Two-Backed Beast, or The Critic Makes the Film, The (Bull), 24, 155
Tynan, Kenneth, 52

Uppercase Print (Jude), 122

Van Sant, Gus, 133
Varda, Agnès, 75, 145
Variety, 82
Verhoeven, Paul, 153
Vertigo (Hitchcock), 53

Village Voice, The, 39, 77, 82-83, 96, 107
Viridiana (Buñuel), 108
Vivre sa vie (Godard), 20
Vlady, Marina, 86
von Stroheim, Erich, 86, 145

Walker, Alexander, 48
Walker, Beverly, 102
Wallace, George, 18, 88
Walsh, Raoul, 48
Wang, Patrick, 159
Warhol, Andy, 147
Wasserman, Lew, 126
Waters, John, 83
Wavelength (Snow), 49, 79
Wedding, A (Altman), 85
Weekend (Godard), 57
Weinberger, Elliot, 97
Weinstein, Harvey, 109
Weissbluth, Dan, 160
Welles, Beatrice, 126
Welles, Orson, 4, 39-40, 49, 56, 58, 71, 80, 101-102, 124-29, 145, 148
Wenders, Wim, 159
Whale, James, 49
What Maisie Knew (James), 66
Which Way to the Front? (Lewis), 117
White, Armond, 53
White, Rob, 109
Who's That Girl? (Foley), 95
Wide Angle, 82
Wild River (Kazan), 19
Willemen, Paul, 65
Williams, Tennessee, 154
Williams, Tony, 24
Will Success Spoil Rock Hunter? (Tashlin), 32
Wind Will Carry Us, The (Kiarostami), 113
Wilson, David, 47
Wilson, Richard, 71
Wilson, Teddy, 23
Winter Soldier (Winterfilm Collective), 96
Wise Blood (Huston), 129
Wise, Robert, 71
Wollen, Peter, 58-59, 62, 84
Wood, Robin, 50, 64, 82
Wright, Frank Lloyd, 8, 13, 15-16, 59, 115, 159

You Are Not I (Driver), 110
Young One, The (Buñuel), 103
Young, Tracy, 84

Zabriskie Point (Antonioni), 129

www.ingramcontent.com/pod-product-compliance
Lightning Source LLC
Chambersburg PA
CBHW070141080526
44586CB00015B/1788